What Others Say About
How to Master Your Muck!

D1605301

. . . .

"The first step toward fabulousness is deciding what you want out of life. The second is clearing away the emotional baggage that's blocking your way to getting there! And that baggage is usually disguised as clutter— whether it's lurking in your email inbox, your kitchen drawers or in your walk-in closet. In *How to Master Your Muck*, Kathi Burns offers effective strategies for clearing away the slop so you can achieve your goals."

—Clinton Kelly, author of *Freakin' Fabulous*, motivational speaker, host of TLC's *What Not to Wear*

"You can continue to struggle every day for the rest of your life, or you can make a decision today to create a life you love! Read *How to Master Your Muck* and you'll learn how to master the 'muck' that's bogging you down, so you can become the master of your destiny—and have more fun getting there!"

—Donna Smallin, author of *A to Z Storage Solutions* and *The One-Minute Organizer*

"How to Master Your Muck is an outstanding resource. It not only helps you organize and simplify your business, it helps you transform it into an enjoyable enterprise. A valuable read!"
> —Standolyn Robertson, President, National Association of Professional Organizers (NAPO)

"Kathi Burns is a fellow change agent. Her new book, *How to Master Your Muck* can help you to begin to create space for changes that you wish to make in your life. I highly recommend this book."
> —Ariane de Bonvoisin, author of *The First 30 Days*

"Based on 30 years in the organizing industry, I am confident that everyone has the potential to create and maintain organizing systems that meet their personal style and needs. Kathi provides simple techniques you can begin to use immediately to increase your results and peace of mind!"
> —Barbara Hemphill, author of *Taming the Paper Tiger at Home*

"Clutter seeps into almost every dimension of our lives—from overflowing closets and stuffed file cabinets to inboxes running out of storage capacity and chaotic schedules. In *How to Master Your Muck*, Kathi expertly guides readers on their journeys to free up their lives, both externally and internally. Of course, this process of trading unruly mess for organizational harmony involves so much more than sorting clothes and canned goods—it also requires an emotional due diligence that Burns is well-acquainted with as a professional organizer."

—Jess Wangsness, *CLOSETS Magazine*

"A successful entrepreneur herself, Kathi Burns shares her creative professional organizing and image consulting expertise for the benefit of all entrepreneurs. You may just find that the best way to start your own dreaded organizing project is with the pleasant task of buying a new pair of shoes!"

—Valentina Sgro, author of the *Patience Oaktree Professional Organizer* book series

"Kathi presents a cogent and compelling argument for lightening up and letting go. In these pages, you will be invited to consider and address the various types of blocks that hold you back from change. Real world stories inspire you to see what is truly possible when you get organized."

—Vicki Norris, Organizing and Life Management Expert and President of Vicki Norris' Restoring Order®

"Dare I say everyone should have a 'muck master' . . . and might I add 'Let it be Kathi Burns!' Kathi's book is the best place to begin that process."

—Dorothy Breininger, CEO, Delphi Center for Organization

"Getting unstuck is easier when you know you're not alone and you have a plan. Kathi gives you both in this handy book, offering specific tips to add space and illustrating her points with insightful stories."
—Porter Knight, Certified Professional Organizer®, author of *Organized to Last*

"Kathi shines the way for you to begin taking control and transforming your life. Even if you don't have a clue where to begin, her book makes it really easy to get started and take action—a wonderful resource!"
—Elizabeth Hagen, CPO®, Organizing Expert/Speaker

"Kathi nails the muck that gets you stuck and tackles it with her eloquent language, powerful systems, and real life examples. *How to Master Your Muck* has the solutions that make taking the step from stuck to unstuck from your muck simple!"
—Patty Kreamer, CPO®, Speaker, Author.
Kreamer Connect, Inc.

"This book will change your life. Kathi's fresh approach will help you with the overwhelming task of clearing your clutter and creating a life that really matters. I highly recommend Kathi's message and applaud her passion to serve."
—Marla Dee, President, Clear & SIMPLE, Inc.
Author of *Get Organized, the Clear & SIMPLE Way*

How to Master
Your Muck

How to Master Your Muck

Get Organized.

Add Space
to Your Life.

Live Your
Purpose!

By Kathi Burns, CPO®

Lemongrass
PUBLISHING

Lemongrass Publishing™
PO Box 232066
Leucadia, California 92023-2066
www.LemongrassPublishing.com

First Edition 2009
Printed in the United States of America

Cover & book design by CenterPointe Media
www.CenterPointeMedia.com

Photography by Jim Volkert
www.JimVolkertPhotography.com

Hair & makeup by Lisa Knight
www.OrangeSalonEncinitas.com

ISBN: 978-0-9819554-0-7
Library of Congress Control Number: 2009902194

Dedication

. . . .

To my true love and dearest friend, Robert Burns. As a husband, your unwavering love and support gives me the time and the courage to explore and discover what I am meant to do in this world. As a business partner, your incredible vision and talents in design, photography and marketing have defined the branding of *addSpace To Your Life!*.

To my mother, Mary Alice Williams. You showed me with your natural flair that it isn't always money that makes great style. It is about your creativity and intention. I miss you oodles.

To my father, Rev. John B. Williams, I am grateful for all of your creative organizing processes! You taught me that it is possible to create a customized system for anything. Your *systems within systems* used to drive me crazy, but I now have to admit, that I learned from the best. Fruit really doesn't fall far from the tree!

To my sister, Joy, and brother, Mike, whose compassion, sincerity and integrity are a continuing source of inspiration.

To Lynne Snow, who proved to me that what comes from love can manifest into something truly magnificent. I know that you are enjoying a new peace that is truly spacious and spectacular!

Table of Contents

. . . .

Preface
• Page XV •

Mastering your external environment is really about changing your mental space. Creating space is a requirement for change.

Introduction
• Page XIX •

The act of mastering, organizing and creating space in your outside world and your relationship with that world is far more potent than you can begin to imagine.

Chapter One
Master Your Papers!

• Page 1 •

Piles of papers represent indecision, procrastination and avoidance. Learn skills and create strategies to take control of your papers and make space for your creativity and passion.

Chapter Two

Consolidate and Master Your Office Supplies

• Page 35 •

Americans waste more than nine million hours each day looking for lost and misplaced articles. Learn how to avoid buying unnecessary duplicate items and stop wasting valuable time every day.

Chapter Three

Mastering Your Home Office

• Page 49 •

Treat your business like a business and invest in business-caliber tools. Make sure your desk has all tools within arm's reach.

Chapter Four

Business Contacts Mastery

• Page 61 •

Project yourself in the world as organized, efficient and professional. Learn how to put your finger on the relevant information you need now.

Chapter Five

Become the Master of Your Inbox

• Page 75 •

Do you feel like emails control your day? Don't get sucked into email oblivion. Become the master of your inbox. Learn how to apply simple rules to maintain proper email etiquette. Keep your focus and take your business to the next level.

Chapter Six
How to Let Go and Master Your Schedule
• Page 91 •

Time is a finite resource. When your schedule is overbooked, minutes and hours evaporate each day from your life. As you let go of all that does not serve you, you will become more successful in less time.

Chapter Seven
Mastering Your Goals Through Thought, Speech and Action
• Page 109 •

If you feel like you are constantly on the move and never getting anywhere, give your unconscious mind a visible path to your goal. Think about how your success will look, speak about it as if it is already real and take action to make things happen.

Chapter Eight
Create a Masterful Image
• Page 123 •

Your appearance impacts your life more than you realize. Your clothes create your first impression and affect how you feel. Create a purposeful image and show how unique and magnificent you truly are!

Chapter Nine

Masters Hire Other Masters

• Page 145 •

Sometimes mastering your own muck can feel overwhelming. You might not know where or how to start. Professionals see where your real blocks lie and help remove them, which creates the space for an inner transformation. Working with other masters will help you master new skills and follow true passions.

Chapter Ten

A Masterful Calling

• Page 155 •

Professional Organizers and Image Consultants help people move through far greater personal obstacles than physical clutter or clothes that don't flatter. The work of professional organizers and image consultants supports the evolution of human consciousness.

About the Author

• Page 165 •

Acknowledgements

• Page 167 •

Notes

• Page 169 •

Preface

. . . .

Muck can be a whole lot of things—your belief systems, old habits that no longer serve you, clutter, a crazy schedule, muddled thinking or an outmoded image. Whatever your muck is, there are tried, true and dependable methods to get unstuck. This book addresses the most common areas where many of my clients get stuck: paper piles, time management, technology stalemates and more. I am here to help you clear the stuff that is holding you back and keeping you from reaching your most fulfilled and thrilling life.

Being stuck has much larger ramifications than being slowed down or even put to a standstill; sometimes you might even go backwards. Have you ever noticed how all your systems depend on each other and everything affects everything else? For instance, you decide to clear out your hall closet. You start emptying the contents

> This book addresses the most common areas where many of my clients get stuck: paper piles, time management, technology stalemates and more.

Muck is a powerful saboteur of creative expression. When you are stuck, it is difficult to bring your unique gifts to the world.

and begin to realize that most of the contents belong in other parts of your house. You are really motivated and decide to move things to where they really belong. You start with the five extra pairs of shoes that you left on the floor of the closet. You head off to your bedroom and oops! there isn't any space in the closet that is their rightful home. Now you are in a quandary, peering into your closet and wondering how in the world you can manage to get your extra shoes stored inside without first straightening out your closet.

Your motivation dissolves. You decide that you just do not have time to tackle all of the areas involved with cleaning out the hall closet, return to the hall closet, place the items back inside and close the door. How long do you think this unfinished project will linger in your mind? I would wager that you would spend weeks thinking that you need to get back in there and finish what you started. Your mind will create many unpleasant thoughts around your organizational skills and you may criticize yourself for months. Additionally, you will dread opening the hall closet door because it reminds you of yet another abandoned task that you would just as soon forget.

Being stuck in the muck can become a roadblock to your success. Muck is a powerful saboteur of creative expression. When you are stuck, it is difficult to bring your unique gifts to the world—you often become frustrated or face financial failure. Muck blocks your ability to be free and follow your heart to live your passion. Clearing the muck or the broken systems in your life will help you learn how to change gracefully and with less effort than you can imagine.

This book reveals two secrets of Professional Organizers and Image Consultants. The first is that changing something outside such as your office environment or physical appearance catalyzes transformation of your inner self. Change creates the space needed for creativity to flourish.

The second and more powerful secret is that a small, seemingly insignificant change in a physical environment can produce a result in your life experience way out of proportion to the size of the act. Just one simple change can open your life in ways you could never imagine.

Don't think of this as a quick fix. Change can be simple but it's not easy, which is why you are reading this book. You need the tools and a way to approach the job that will align with your creative potential.

My joy in life is working with people who want to remove obstacles to create change in their life, because, as a serial change artist, I truly know who you are and how I might help. I thrive on riding the waves of change and actively co-create the new chapters of my life as

A small, seemingly insignificant change in a physical environment can produce a result in your life experience way out of proportion to the size of the act.

they unfold. I know that I can manifest good into my life by remaining open, spacious and receptive enough to allow new ideas to enter.

Improving organizational processes can be a special challenge for people creating themselves anew in this fast-paced world. After working with thousands of clients, I know you have the ability to think outside the box and that you also have the potential to create and maintain organizing systems that will work uniquely for you. Organizing does not have to be tedious: it is a truly creative endeavor.

I will shine the light for you to make changes and take charge of your life, business and the systems within. Right now, you are resonating with this book because your current methods have fallen short of your true potential.

I am holding the way for you; I have the vision and knowledge that you can accomplish and maintain any change that you desire. I KNOW this to be true for you . . . as it was true for me. So let's have some fun and figure out where to start.

Namaste,[1]
Kathi

Introduction

. . . .

"Change is the law of life. And those who look only to the past or present are certain to miss the future."[2]
—John F. Kennedy

Change is my true nature and it brings me great joy.

I was actually surprised to discover that change is often very difficult for others to embrace. My fearlessness and the sense of joy that I feel while enabling change is a unique and valuable skill that I now use to help others. I also know that where there is a newly cleared space, there is an instant opportunity for change.

Space always brings clarity. This is why I named my company *addSpace to Your Life!*. When you have the advantage of extra space and time, you can see clearly what you need to do to manifest a successful and fulfilling

> When you have the advantage of extra space and time, you can see clearly what you need to do to manifest a successful and fulfilling life.

life. This might be why many of us have a strong desire to meditate or pray: it gives our brains a chance to add space, pause and reflect. To see this principle in your physical environment, try this simple exercise: move your desk a few feet from the wall. You will see clearly what you need to do that your vacuum cleaner did not. You might also decide that now that you have a new vantage point, you might prefer to reposition your desk within the room. This also works in your life. Move a few things around, whether it is in your schedule or your closet, and you will also begin to see more clearly what you need to do to get unstuck and express your true nature.

Outwardly removing a few of these blocks will create a much deeper and subtle inner impact on your life than you would ever anticipate. The actual act of organizing or creating more order/space in your outside world and your relationship with that world is far more potent than you can imagine. Once your blocks are removed, you will have more time, confidence and freedom to do what you love. You will be able to step out into your full glory and manifest your life as expressed through your joy and your passions. I have witnessed this firsthand as my clients develop and nurture their true talents.

People often become attached to thoughts, habits, piles and—believe it or not—broken systems. These

> Once your blocks are removed, you will have more time, confidence and freedom to do what you love.

> According to Rabbi Louis Binstock, *"Very often we are our own worst enemy as we foolishly build stumbling blocks on the path that leads to success and happiness."*

attachments can become blocks. Your blocks might include paperwork or losing track of important business connections. It might also be the way in which you present yourself to the world through your wardrobe. I have two clients who demonstrate this principle in action. And there are many other clients (their names have been changed to honor their privacy) whose stories are featured throughout this book.

Changing Your Old Beliefs

Thomas illustrates how powerful thoughts become blocks and seemingly unrelated clearing can release huge obstacles. He called one day to request that I update his wardrobe and image to help him shift his life. He said that he owned a private dental practice and that he had been trying for a year on his own to make changes in his business and lifestyle to reflect his artistic passions and decided that if he could start with his outward appearance, other things might also shift for him. A very intuitive client indeed!

One of the most striking things I discovered in my client's wardrobe was his pair of black Reebok high-top tennis shoes. Remember the style? They were easily 10 years old, with cracks across the soles. He wore these shoes every day from work to home to gym—literally everywhere. I knew immediately that one of my goals was to move him into better shoes. After all, as they say, shoes make the man.

Our day of shopping arrived. After finding several fabulous clothing items, we moved onto shoes. As he tried on several pairs, he said, "Oh, I didn't know buckle shoes were back in" and then remained quiet for a while as he tried on more styles. We didn't find the perfect shoe just then so we continued on to other stores. As we walked, he had an epiphany. "You know, I am just now remembering an event from when I was a teenager," he told me. "I had worked really hard one summer and saved up my money. In the fall, I saw these great black buckle shoes and decided to buy them. They were better than any shoes I had ever owned and I thought they were fantastic! They also took all of the money I had saved but I was very proud of them and came home to show my parents.

When I showed up wearing my new shoes, my father said, 'Why would you waste your money on something like that? You have perfectly respectable shoes that I bought for you two years ago.' My mother was mortified and said they were really an eyesore.

I left the house and decided that, no matter, I was going to keep the shoes. I'll tell you though, after that I didn't feel quite as cool wearing them. I hadn't thought about that until now when I see all of these buckle shoes."

After hearing that story, I suddenly realized why Thomas had been wearing those old Reeboks for years. He had held onto the inherited values of his parents and chose to keep his shoes long past their prime just like he had subconsciously held onto the family values that no longer served him.

Here he was, a successful dentist with his own thriving practice, wearing shoes with cracks across the soles every day of his life.

It wasn't about the amount of money the shoes cost, it was about the value he placed on himself.

I knew that what Thomas needed most was a pair of incredibly fabulous new shoes. We started trying on $70 shoes, moved into $200 shoes, and finally found a pair of $540 Italian leather shoes! After much dialogue and introspection, my client was finally ready to step into a new pair of shoes and claim new ideas about what was possible in his life.

For this man seeking to shift his outmoded life, the next step was literally stepping into a new pair of shoes. It wasn't about the amount of money the shoes cost, it was about the value he placed on himself. He was truly worthy of a pair of handcrafted Italian shoes!

It's been almost four years now, and I still shop for Thomas. He called me recently to help him find some new jeans and casual slacks. He said, "I need a new pair of jeans, not just any type of jeans, something really unique and unusual." Go figure! Create a Masterful Image is a bonus chapter and prequel to my upcoming book that will include more techniques to master your image.

Thomas has since sold his private practice, manifested a cushy job as a dentist in the Navy, shows his art in galleries and is the winner of several awards for his photography. I think that a major shift happened for this gentleman. Would you agree?

Making Space For the New

An interesting email arrived early one morning. It read:

"I've tried many things over the years to help my daughter. She is an aspiring actor and has been chronically disorganized for years. I am suspicious that it is causing a number of failures in her life. I found your website this worrisome and sleepless night at 4:00 a.m. I have been trying to help my daughter and have been sponsoring talk therapy. I have begun to realize that our daughter sitting on a sofa in a therapist's office talking about her problems is too far removed from the actual things weighing her down. I think that our adult daughter needs practical hands-on intervention."

My heart ached reading this story from a very wise mother. I scheduled an appointment as soon as I could and began working with her daughter a few weeks later. I quickly discovered that there were many things weighing her down and that she was living the quintessential life of the starving artist. We started clearing, sorting, and organizing her mounds of papers and clothes, including getting her excess possessions out of storage and into her apartment. She had moved from L.A. to San Diego without taking inventory or clearing her life in advance. Many items had ended up in storage by default as she transitioned into a much smaller apartment. At that point, she was teaching acting and working as a bartender between acting jobs.

The significant challenge was this: her life was too chaotic and she didn't have enough space to even begin to consider the goals required to realize her dreams. She was constantly on the run, running for money and running for small acting parts. Her manuscripts were in disarray. It took hours to find the scripts she needed for her students. Her finances were jumbled because she had never stopped to learn how to organize a budget. She truly believed that life had simply happened to her and that she had no control over the outcome. Her real dream was to move to New York City and jump-start her career.

> ...her life was too chaotic and she didn't have enough space to even begin to consider the goals required to realize her dreams. She was constantly on the run...

After we cleared her excess clothes and created order in her personal paperwork and scripts, we could begin working with her time and money management. It became clear that she would need to shift her employment to a day job to create the space and flexibility to be fresh for last-minute auditions and have the ability to work them if she got the parts. Once we earmarked a timeline for her move to the Big Apple, we plotted a budget to determine what she would need so that she would have enough money to move and cover rent and expenses to survive two to three months while she looked for new employment.

I am happy to report that she arrived in New York only one month behind schedule and is happily pursuing her quest for an acting career. When she moved, she did not carry many of her past problems in physical form. Her mother wrote to me later, "Her life is running much smoother and I feel that she is in a much better place to succeed."

The Way Forward

Navigating your way through life might seem overly complex with roadblocks on every level. Simplifying your life by releasing clutter and old patterns will pave the way for success. The best place for you to start will be to nudge and budge your most persistent block. Get

Simplifying your life by releasing clutter and old patterns will pave the way for success.

rid of the biggest monkey on your back and you will see very clearly what to do next.

Be willing to change your attitude about change—learn to embrace a new perspective. You will soon be open to new possibilities and able to create your life based on your true skills and passions.

> **Remember:** A rather small, seemingly insignificant change will often propel you into larger-than-life results.

The change can begin in your home or business. It doesn't really matter where you begin, every environment where you live, work and breathe affects every other.

This book can save you a lot of time as you work through your changes. You may only need to read one chapter. As a busy person on the move, I realize that your time is valuable and also probably limited. To help you identify what you should read, I have strategically placed three thought-provoking questions at the beginning of each chapter. Read these questions first. This will help you determine where you should start.

If you resonate with all three questions at the beginning of a chapter, consider reading that chapter first. If you resonate with two out of the questions, I suggest that you definitely read that chapter next. If you resonate with only one question in a chapter, you should read it only after you delve into the more urgent challenges that are currently and directly affecting your life. If you are still unsure where to begin, start with Chapter One, "Master Your Papers!" This is an area where 95% of all people need guidance. Please use the large margins on each page if you want to jot down notes to yourself.

The reality is this—you have the capacity for huge change and the ability to manifest everything that you desire. Know this in your heart and move forward boldly. After all, the one constant factor in life is change. As Buddha stated, "Everything changes, nothing remains without change."[3] Anais Nin also wrote poetically about the inevitability of change, "Life is a process of becoming, a combination of states we have to go through. Where people fail is that they wish to elect a state and remain in it. This is a kind of death."

Do not let your dreams die: move forward and learn the new skills necessary to uncover and discover your true talents so that you can bring them forth. The world is waiting for you to step out in your full glory, and I am eagerly anticipating your success. I will shine the light for you while you create a life that truly follows your passion!

> The reality is this—you have the capacity for huge change and the ability to manifest everything that you desire.

Chapter One

**Master
Your
Papers!**

"A good paper filing
system makes it easy for
you to move your papers
in, through and—most
importantly—out of your
environment."

Read This Chapter First If You Resonate With These Questions:

Is your office and/or desk inundated with paperwork?

. . . .

Do you feel stressed because you can't find important papers when you need them?

. . . .

Do you have two or more mystery piles on your desk right now? These are random stacks of notes, lists, mail and other papers that keep growing until you have no idea what's in the piles.

If you feel overwhelmed by the deluge of paper in your life, you are not alone. Most people today are coping with an unprecedented flood of paper —invoices, bills, receipts, flyers, notices, contracts, receipts, to-do lists and correspondence of all sorts. According to research conducted by the nonprofit organization 41pounds.org, U.S. companies send out an estimated 62 billion pieces of junk mail each year. This means that every American adult receives an average of 41 pounds of junk mail annually.[4]

If you don't have an easy, effective system for organizing your papers, you're probably spending a lot of time looking for that lost invoice or contract—time that you could be doing the work you love and creating more income.

In fact, according to a recent Esselte study, the average U.S. executive wastes six weeks each year looking for important documents lost in the clutter of his or her office (or car, briefcase, kitchen . . .) For an employee who earns an annual salary of $60,000, that time costs the company a staggering $6,290. If you are an entrepreneur, I know you don't want to waste more than $6,000 every year simply because you are disorganized. Imagine all of the things you could do with that money!

In addition to saving yourself time and money, creating an effective filing system protects the business you've worked so hard to create. Paperwork and files are not only the largest burden for small businesses—they are very often the glue that holds the entire business together. According to a study by World-Scan, more than 70% of today's businesses would fail within three weeks if they suffered a catastrophic loss of paper-based records due to fire or flood. In many ways, paperwork is a vital business asset.

The value of having a good filing system was underscored for business owners and many others during the 2007 fires that destroyed thousands of homes and buildings in San Diego. Many of my clients had to flee their home offices due to imminent danger, and those who had implemented a new filing system emailed me later with heartfelt thanks. They not only knew what their important papers were, they knew exactly where to run grab them as they vacated their property.

After the fires, one client wrote me this note: "When we evacuated for the fire this year, my new filing system saved me much time and stress. I was able to pull all permanent files and policies with all my insurance information. I grabbed and grabbed and ran out, knowing that I had everything I could possibly want. A few years ago when we had to evacuate, we just grabbed memorabilia and didn't even think of anything else besides insurance policies. I did not know where things were so I didn't even think of it. This time I had all of the important information."

Clearing the Space for Creativity

Although organizing your papers might seem like a dry, boring task, it is, in fact, a crucial step that will allow you to tap into your deepest creative potential. It is therefore well worth the effort. Right now, you may not realize how much your energy is being drained by the chaos in this area of your life. Even if you aren't aware of it, being disorganized is stressful, filling your mind with niggling thoughts about whether you remembered to pay a bill, make plane reservations, or send out an invoice. Ultimately, this is a drain on your creative reserves and your ability to focus on growing a successful business.

The story of my client, Carla, illustrates the powerful freedom and confidence that comes from getting unstuck from the muck of paper disorganization. When I first met Carla at a conference, she firmly believed that she needed to move into a larger house to accommodate her growing business as an author, coach and professional speaker.

As a cancer survivor, she had spent years battling to get well, while the organization of her business and personal life fell apart. When she went into remission, she faced the chaotic jumble of papers that had literally taken over her home and office. She told me that she felt desperate and truly believed that she needed to find a larger house.

Even without seeing Carla's home, I knew that if she could gain control of her paperwork, she would find a lot of extra space. As we began working together, I saw that she had a bit more than papers to clear in her life; she also had old habits that had overwhelmed her home and office with clutter. There were piles of papers covering every horizontal surface available.

Carla dreaded the thought of tackling the mess and compared it to the pain of getting her teeth drilled, but she stuck with the process. After working together to set up a paper flow system, she now has newly created open space within her home and office, and she has decided that not having a paper file system for eight years was similar to having a terminal illness with no hope for the future.

> "Facing an obstacle like paper clutter and disorganization has been very freeing," she said. "Like any new habit, it takes discipline and has to be addressed continuously. I definitely know a new freedom in being able to throw away stuff immediately and now live in an environment with cleared tables and desktops. This is a lovely feeling—well worth the 'teeth drilling' pain of transformation!"

Letting go of old habits and facing change may feel uncomfortable or even painful at first, but if you can allow yourself to move forward despite the discomfort, you will find more joy, freedom and transformation. I have seen hundreds of clients overcome paper clutter and know that you can do it too. In this chapter, I will guide you in a step-by-step process for creating an effective file system that will move obsolete papers out of your life and keep important documents in action at your fingertips. Let's get started!

The Paper Action Plan

I will provide a more detailed explanation of each of these steps as we go along, but this summary offers a map of where we are going:

1. Toss and Sort.

2. Choose Your Paper Filing System.

3. Organize Your Action Papers.

4. Work Your Action Papers: Maintain the Flow.

Suggested Tools to Have on Hand to Create Your New File System

1. Freedom Filer filing system[5]

2. **Eight boxes of army-green hanging file folders**, with 1/5th-cut clear tabs.[6] If you buy these at a store, make sure that the tabs are bent or angled; in other words, not straight up and down when viewed from the side. The bend allows you to read the tabs from above the file folder when files are placed in the bottom drawer of a cabinet. If they are not bent, you will not be able to read the tabs in the bottom drawer without physically bending them with your finger to read from above. The reason to purchase army green folders is that they always come with clear tabs. There is no need to buy colored folders and you probably should not, because colored folders are typically packaged with colored tabs that make it impossible to read the Freedom Filer colored labels. This system already is color-coded and you don't want to give your brain mixed signals. To save aggravation and time, buy eight boxes of file folders. *You will really use that many and maybe more.*

An interesting fact: With Freedom Filer, you wind up with more files and less paper.

3. 10 to 30 manila folders *(make sure you have clean, crisp folders)*[7]

You will use these for your desktop Action Folders.

4. Stepped vertical-file holder[8]

These units are generally made from plastic-coated metal in black or chrome. Make sure it has eight steps or compartments and is designed as an ascending vertical staircase. You will need two file holders if you are creating both a home and a business file system.

5. One pack of banker's boxes[9]

These are generally sold in packs of four or five boxes. You will need a minimum of four boxes to hold your sorted papers until you finish assembling your files and determine which drawers they should be moved into.

6. Other handy items to have on hand: Sticky notepads (Post-its), stapler and paperclips.

Step One:
Toss and Sort Your Papers

Begin by designating five empty file-folder box lids, one for each of the following categories: Action, Permanent,

Tax, Resources and Policies. Now grab a large trashcan and get busy sorting. Toss the unimportant papers directly into the trash, recycle or shred bin. Sort the rest of the papers into one of the other categories:

Action Papers

These are papers that require your immediate attention, such as bills, a reminder to renew your driver's license, an RSVP you need to send or other such items.

Permanent Files

Permanent records include certificates, education and medical records, family history or genealogy and memorabilia. This category also includes permanent property records such as titles, original purchase receipts, maintenance receipts and warranties. As a general rule, permanent records for property include any papers relevant to the resale of the property. Permanent corporate records include articles of incorporation, stock certificates, corporate minutes, etc.

References/Resources

These are the papers that you reference for your business or home. It might be brochures, industry trend reports or fact sheets. Personal reference papers might range from how to grow roses to health and fitness routines.

Before you decide to save articles, clippings, notes, brochures and literature for future reference, consider that more current information is likely to be available at a later time on the Internet or by making a phone call. For example, rather than saving travel brochures, you can always browse online or call a travel agent to get the most up-to-date information when the time comes to plan your trip. If there is an article you wish to read, consider placing it with your action file system instead of creating a file folder. If you don't end up reading it, chances are you never will. Recipes may be kept in a binder in the kitchen, and magazines are best kept near the places where you enjoy reading.

Policies

The easiest way to determine whether a piece of paper falls into the policy category is to ask yourself if it is an agreement with the world. For instance, my Social Security statement is a policy because it is an agreement between the U.S. government and me. The government has agreed to pay me a certain amount each month upon my retirement. Other policy examples include leases, home loans, rental agreements, wills, service provider contracts and employment benefits packages—and even your current résumé.

Many policies and documents are periodically

updated, renewed or replaced. This means that every time you receive a new policy, the old one is no longer valid and can be thrown out or shredded. However, there are some exceptions. For example, your expired homeowner's policy might be best kept in a permanent home records file in case of unnoticed damage such as a rainwater leak. If you refinance or sell your home, keep the prior mortgage agreement with your tax records for 10 years. If there is an outstanding claim or dispute regarding any policy or contract, keep the documents with your active files until resolved. Afterwards, you can file receipts showing compensation with your tax records. Repair records may be kept in a permanent file for the person or property concerned. Policies is a very liberating category because it teaches me what to throw out. The top of the tab reads Remove/Replace and automatically reminds me to throw out the old when I add something new. I love this category!

Policies is a very liberating category because it teaches me what to throw out.

Tax-Related Documents

Set aside any tax-related documents you accumulate during the year in a separate box. These might include medical expenses, charitable contributions, business bank statements or supplies. If you have more than one year of saved papers when you sort, separate these papers into individual years. If you are unsure which papers to keep or toss, and you are conducting the same type of business this year as last, refer to your most recent tax return to see what paper records were required. If unsure or working at a new business, contact a CPA to determine your categories and adapt your tax folders later. Creating accurate categories will help speed up your tax preparation in the following years. Freedom Filer is set up to mimic your tax return categories, and later you will separate your current receipts into these categories.

Note: If you use software to categorize tax-related expenses, you may file receipts by month, or by vendor A-Z, in a designated tax area, separated from personal bills and receipts.

To Toss or Not to Toss? The 80/20 Pareto Principle Also Applies to Paper

Many people hire a Professional Organizer because they have accumulated so much paper that they could never get it sorted out on their own. Over the years, they have stashed papers in boxes, bins and file cabinets, but can't find any of it when they need it. If you feel overwhelmed by your clutter, please see the resource chapter in the back to locate a Professional Organizer in your area.[10]

The Pareto Principle, also known as the 80/20 Rule, states that a small number of causes (20%) are responsible for a large percentage (80%) of the effect. What this means for your paperwork is that only 20% of the papers on your desk and in your office are actually necessary to perform your job. The other 80% are the clutter that form your mystery piles and make it difficult to stay focused on your priorities.

If you are organizing your papers on your own, keep in mind that it pays to be ruthless and toss as many papers as possible during this part of the process. It will make your life easier and save you a lot of time later on. When you look at an item, ask yourself: *Is this article on networking (or websites, raising puppies, or any other piece of information) something that I can easily find online? Will I be able to quickly access more current information if I need it in the future?* If your answer is yes, don't waste time saving and filing it. It is more important to spend your energy creating files for irreplaceable items like client testimonials and tax returns. By remembering that 80% of filed papers are never retrieved, you probably will be able to throw out more papers than you file.

Also, don't worry about determining the specific folder headings at this time; simply place it into one of the categories above: Reference, Policies, Tax-Related or Permanent files. Use one of your new hanging folder box lids or a simple Post-it note placed on the desk above each pile.

Step Two:
Choose Your Paper Filing System

A good paper system makes it easy for you to move your papers in, through, and—most importantly—*out* of your environment. It will be easily sustainable and endurable over the years as your life changes, and it will enable you to get more done in less time.

As a Certified Professional Organizer, I've used a variety of filing systems, and over the years have found Freedom Filer to be the best paper filing system on the market. In fact, the paper flow system laid out in this chapter is based on the Freedom Flier kit, used with gracious permission by its creator, Seth Odam.

You can build your new filing system on your own using the information in this book or get a jump-start and purchase a Freedom Filer kit (which costs a little under $50). I have constructed more than 300 filing systems for various clients using the Freedom Filer kit, and it is completely adaptable, whether you run multiple corporations or simply need a system to organize your sole proprietorship or personal files.

A good paper system makes it easy for you to move your papers in, through, and—most importantly— *out* of your environment.

You can learn more about the Freedom Filer in the resource section of this book, but I'll briefly describe the highlights here:

- Freedom Filer includes pre-printed color-coded labels for the main file categories (Reference, Tax-related, Policies and Permanent), as well as hundreds of other specific labels and blank labels that allow you to customize your filing system to your specific needs.

- The kit contains illustrated instructions and handy reference index cards that make it easy to quickly set up your files and keep them organized.

- The files are both color-coded and alphabetical, which makes it easy to retrieve documents.

What I like most about Freedom Filer is that it is designed to be "self-purging"; that is, it has a built-in system that lets you know when to remove papers from your files and either toss them or rotate them to other file categories. The system prevents file "bloating"—the accumulation of papers you no longer need, as well as the common phenomenon of file entropy, file cabinets becoming more and more disorganized over time as papers are misfiled and forgotten.

Step Three:
Organize Your Action Papers

Once you have tossed the unimportant papers, picked your filing system and separated your papers into major categories and lids, it is time to begin organizing your most critical papers, those that require you to take some type of action.

Pick up a single piece of paper at a time unless it is already grouped by staple or paperclip. Think about what type of action is required first to begin working on it.

When you begin to sort your Action papers, it helps to think in terms of the baby steps you'll need to take to complete whatever action is needed. For example, if you are looking at a bill, perhaps the first action you need to take is to phone the creditor for more information about an unclear charge. The next action might involve waiting for a response to your question. After you receive the return call, you then need to enter the data, i.e., make a note of the information in your records. Finally, you submit your payment. Using this method, your Action papers will probably move around your file system until they are complete.

Action Paper Categories

Calls to Make	:	Coupons/Certificates
Bills to Pay	:	Upcoming Events
Waiting for Response	:	Meetings, to Discuss
Current Projects	:	Outbound to Others
Data Entry	:	

Calls to Make

Everyone has phone calls that they need to make in order to follow up or initiate activities. Keep notes with names and numbers in this folder so that you can make all of your calls at once to optimize your time.

Bills to Pay

When you retrieve your mail, instead of dropping it onto your kitchen counter, it's easy to separate the bills

addSpace **TIPS** Call your creditors to see if you can arrange to have all of your bills due on the same day of each month. If your budget does not permit this, ask if they can adjust the due dates to either the 1st and the 15th or the 5th and the 20th. If your bills are grouped into one to two periods during the month, you will only have to spend time paying them once or twice each month. If the due dates are spread out throughout the month, your bills will arrive almost every day, and you will spend more time opening, filing and paying them.

and put them into your bills folder. When it comes time to pay bills, open the folder and write the checks or pay online all at once.

Waiting for Response

Most of the time, you're probably waiting to hear back from at least one person or business for one reason or another. Maybe it is the cable company about a billing issue or the lawn guy with a new estimate. Whatever it is, make a note or drop the related paper into this folder and you will stay on top of your affairs effortlessly.

Current Projects

The Current Projects folder is really the heart of the system. Everyone has projects in process. Maybe it is writing a new business plan or updating your website. Whatever it is, this folder provides a handy place to keep your papers related to projects. Don't be surprised if your current projects end up using two of your vertical steps. This is another reason I insist on eight-stepped sections even though you might not have eight folder titles—it gives you the latitude to keep track of multiple projects while still keeping them vertical and off of your desktop.

When a project starts, it might only be one piece of paper and can stay in the Current Projects folder. Over time, it might warrant an entire separate folder labeled with the name of the project. When this happens, simply place the new project folder behind the Current Projects folder, and you will know right where to find it!

Data Entry

There is always incoming information that you need to enter into your handy computer database. Maybe it is a new address, a birthday, or the name of a new book that you want to put on your "to read" list. Whatever it is, drop your notes into your Data Entry folder and when you have several, enter the information in one sitting to save time. (The upcoming database chapter will explain how to use your computer contact management program to keep your contacts organized and working for you.)

Coupons/Gift Certificates

This file provides a handy place to deposit your gift cards, vouchers and coupons and makes it easier to remember to actually use them!

Uncover Your Buried Treasures

Did you know that gift cards are one of the most lucrative inventory items for stores? This is because less than 60% of the gift cards purchased are actually redeemed for merchandise. Gift cards and certificates are frequently lost under piles and stuffed into the bottom of drawers. Almost every client I work with finds at least one gift card that he or she had tucked away and forgotten about. One of my clients was a schoolteacher who found 22 gift cards valued at more than $1,200 when we organized her home. This is not unusual; in fact, most people find money, checks, or gift cards when they organize their home with a Professional Organizer. The largest find I've seen so far was my client who found $4,700 in uncashed checks, stock certificates and gift cards. Now you can see why it pays to get organized!

Meetings, to Discuss

Keep this folder in action throughout your week, dropping notes in to remind yourself about questions you need to ask during upcoming meetings, or topics you would like to discuss. This practice empowers you to use meetings to your best advantage and waste less time in meetings that don't help accomplish your goals. If you attend multiple meetings on a regular basis, make a folder for each meeting and keep these folders on the same-stepped level within your action system.

If you attend several regular meetings that require a lot of paper preparation, consider creating folders with specific headings. Tuck these behind your generic upcoming meetings file on the same-stepped level, making it easy to grab the individual folder as you run out the door to your meeting.

Upcoming Events

This folder is the catchall location for items such as event schedules, class schedules and wedding invitations. This is not the place to keep your regular calendar, which will live on your desk and travel with you. The Upcoming Events folder is simply a holding zone for the information you need for upcoming events, i.e., yoga class schedules, party directions, gift registry info, etc.

Outbound to Others

 This is a great place to keep papers that belong to other people within your company or your home. If you are a soloprenuer, you might also have a *For Spouse* file in your personal action files area.

Keep Your Papers in Action at Your Fingertips

Now that you have sorted your papers into categories, let's focus on the Action papers and set them up so that you can perform your job more efficiently and have more time for fun!

The ideal paper system will have a separate area for each action step. In my experience with clients, I find that the best file frame is a vertical file holder with eight separate steps or sections. This frame will keep your papers off of your desk surface and out of horizontal piles by holding your action folders upright and keeping your most urgent business in full view. You can purchase these file frames at most office supply stores or order them online.[11]

This system provides a way to keep all of your active papers on your desk until they are completed in a space-saving and visually appealing system. As with all good systems, there are exceptions. If there are over 16 files currently "in action," you might consider storing them in the front of the top file drawer within arm's reach of your desk chair. The reason for this is that you never want too many paper files on your desk, especially if you have a limited amount of desk surface. Even if they are organized vertically, if there are too many files, they will overtake your desktop, add visual clutter and distract you. Another exception to the keeping active papers on your desk rule is if you are sensitive to visual clutter, as some of my clients are. If this is the case, action files should be placed in the drawer closest to you. The disadvantage is that you will have to constantly remind yourself to open the drawer and keep an eye on these critical papers.

The third exception is if you run a business and also handle personal bills at the same desk. In this case, you need to have at least a six-foot desk.

I suggest placing two vertical file holders on the desk—one marked *Business* and the other *Personal*. They are best positioned when flanking opposite sides of the computer screen.

Keeping your Action papers organized and directly in your line of sight (preferably beside your computer monitor) is a visual reminder to focus on your highest priority items. Use whichever label titles work best for you and work on these files a few minutes every day.

Step Four:
Work Your Action Folders

Once you have your papers in Action organized and filed vertically, you still need to have a system to keep track of what you need to do. This vertical step file is

Keeping your Action papers organized and directly in your line of sight (preferably beside your computer monitor) is a visual reminder to focus on your highest priority items.

not magic. It does not move papers in and out of your life on its own. It requires a driver, which is you.

Working your Action files and keeping control of your business and life is actually very simple, but it does require ongoing diligence. You have eight steps in your vertical frame representing eight different types of action. If you open at least one of these folders every day during the week, you will see and be aware of every ongoing detail in your life in a week or two.

Working your Action file doesn't mean that you have to do everything in one file folder every day. It does mean, however, that you open the file folder, look through it and do one or two of the items to move them along. The beauty of the system is that you are in charge. You consciously choose what to do now and what can wait until later. Because you look at them regularly, you are fully aware of what still needs to be done, and it doesn't get lost in a pile somewhere.

If you work your Action files properly, nothing important will ever fall through the cracks. It is well worth the effort. Not only will you be in control of your life, the monkeys of worry will slowly release their hold on your subconscious mind, making you more energized, focused and empowered as you go about your day.

Working your Action files and keeping control of your business and life is actually very simple, but it does require ongoing diligence.

Every new practice requires due diligence before it becomes a habit. When you add a new activity to your routine, you need to do it for at least four weeks before it becomes automatic. This means that you have to practice working your Action files every day for at least a month before it becomes a regular part of your work routine.

The hanging files in your file cabinets are used to store the less frequently used categories, such as Permanent records and Policies. In business file systems, the resource file drawer should typically be the one closest to you. As you decide which files to store in which drawer location, consider the frequency with which you will need to access them. Typically, permanent and policy information is accessed less often than resources and would be farther away from your desk chair. If you are using a four-drawer file adjacent to your desk, you should store your most frequently accessed file category in the drawers that are within arm's reach of your chair.

Even Artists Can File

Creative types are so busy creating beauty that they often fail to realize that they have ruined their environment with clutter. One of my clients, Sophia, a fine artist, actually discarded enough paper to fill 32 recycle bins when we created her filing system! Sofia loved fonts, pictures and graphic ideas so deeply that she clipped every great idea and example that she admired in every publication that she came across. After 30 years of collecting these ideas, she could not find them or even use them when needed because they were not organized. They were simply boxed, filed or piled without proper labels. Sophia recently sent me this email; "You are a miracle worker! By teaching me to establish categories for my stuff, you rescued my downward disorganization spiral, turning it into an upward organized one. Objects can now find a 'home.' Pieces of paper can be filed. A couple of new desktop file names are 'data entry' and 'calls to make' really saved me from myself!"

Many artists deplore file cabinets because they are ugly and feel very constraining. While it is true that many file cabinets are not very attractive and take up a great deal of space, a proper filing system in a real filing cabinet is a great remedy for paper clutter. I emphasize the word *proper* because cute or fancy boxes that are marketed as file cabinets but aren't functional seduce many artists. This is not saying that you have to own a whole wall of four-drawer filing cabinets. According to *Office Systems Magazine*, a professional, four-drawer file cabinet holds 18,000 sheets of paper,[12] so you will probably need at least one file cabinet for your business,

> ...a proper filing system in a real filing cabinet is a great remedy for paper clutter.

and an additional one if you wish to keep your personal papers organized in your home office.

Going Paperless? Not in This Decade!

We will never be paperless, at least not anytime soon. A plastic surgeon colleague has worked diligently to create a paperless office. Even though the majority of his files are electronic, he still uses paper for the anesthesiologists. He says that they prefer to use paper for their charts, and he will respect that so as not to sacrifice client care. I find this to be the case in every industry, even virtual workplaces. One of my clients hires and trains virtual assistants in India. She is the most technically savvy person I have encountered. She uses a high-speed scanner and pays all bills online yet still needs a filing system for her office. She has spent much effort scanning and creating computer data files but still finds areas where she needs paper.

We can take steps to reduce our papers by using technology. An important key to this process is acquiring a fast scanner. If you decide to eliminate most of your papers, it will pay to invest in a high-speed scanner (not a flatbed scanner) that can scan a large stack of papers at a time. This way, you can add a stack, wait for it to scan, and then name each file as it imports into your computer. As you import into your computer, you will need an organizing method.

Electronic data storage has similar pitfalls to paper storage. You still need an organized file folder system on your computer so that you can easily retrieve your documents. I find that when the Freedom Filer is in place, it is easy to mimic that file structure on a computer. For instance, you can create computer folders named Resources, Permanent Records and so on. Names and numbers also have to be organized on your computer, and this is where a good contact management program pays off tremendously.

A contact management program is also necessary so that you can set up a reminder system to avoid missing deadlines and opportunities. We will explore contact management programs and how to make full use of your business contacts in the Business Contacts Mastery chapter.

Step Five:
The Beauty of Empty Space:
Keeping Your Desk Clear

Begin by looking at your desk. How much of the surface is cleared? How much room do you have to work? Once you organize your papers, at least 60% of your desktop will be clear. You may also find more open space in your office.

This open surface helps you think more clearly. This means you might also have space for a second chair for guests, and that papers no longer clutter the surface of your desk. This open surface helps you think more clearly. It also helps by providing a place to rest your arms while typing or taking notes and an area to keep your project folder open as you work.

A Real-life Story:
The Half-Decade Filing Routine

A very successful contractor client used to keep his desk loaded with paperwork. Joe used the power of time to purge his papers. When we met, he had four years of papers stacked high over the entire surface of his huge U-shaped desk. His organizing method was the "5-year plan": every five years or so, he would throw away every paper on the surface of his desk and then begin again.

Before we met, Joe thought this was an easier method than making a decision about each piece of paper as he received it.

Fortunately, his large and competent staff made sure that the super important papers were hand-delivered, signed and taken out of his office before they were lost for the next half-decade! As a result, his employees wasted many hours keeping him organized instead of performing their actual jobs. Now that this CEO uses Freedom Filer, he is on top of his paperwork, and his staff no longer has to combat the black hole on his desk. Joe was actually never that concerned about his piles throughout his office, but later he told me: "The reason that I called you in to help me with organizing my papers was peer pressure. Everyone seemed to think that my office was a mess and made comments about it. Quite honestly, I didn't want to have meetings in here either. After we moved all of the old records and banker's boxes into storage, you recommended that I bring in a small meeting table and chairs for one-on-one meetings. Now that I am cleared up and conduct private meetings in here, I get rave reviews about my newfound office space. People seem to be amazed and the comments are now on a positive note."

Always sort your mail over the trash or recycling bin.

Now that you have discovered that only 20% of your papers should be filed, and you have a strategy to file them, you are ready to move on. In the next chapter, we will explore the process of organizing your office supplies. You will learn how to corral your supplies and keep them from overtaking your workspace. You will create areas to store your back-up supplies so that you will no longer have to perform the crazy goose chase to find a new printer cartridge!

addSpace Action Steps

1. Toss old and unnecessary papers.
2. Sort the papers to keep.
3. Choose your file system.
4. Organize your action papers.
5. Work your action papers.

Links to the products referenced in this chapter are available in the Notes section at the end of the book.

• Notes •

Chapter Two

Consolidate and
Master Your
Office Supplies

"You can learn how to create areas to hold back-up supplies so they will not hinder your business at hand."

Read This Chapter First If You Resonate With These Questions:

Do you frequently have to interrupt your creative workflow to find that misplaced toner cartridge, a package of Post-it notes or a pen that works?

. . . .

Do you feel overwhelmed by the piles of supplies that cram your office shelves, yet never seem to find what you want when you need it?

. . . .

Do you get distracted by the stuff piled on your desk and around your office . . . the dirty coffee cup, the package of paper you meant to put away, the printer you need to return to the store?

Knowing where to find your supplies solves two very specific problems:

1. You stop wasting valuable time every day searching for staples, pencils and paper. According to

the American Demographic Society, the search time can add up to over 170 hours per person every year.

2. You stop buying unnecessary duplicate items on a regular basis, which, in turn, saves time and money and creates peace of mind. You will know that at a crucial deadline, you have what you need to complete your project. You will also gain the "plan ahead" advantage and buy things on sale rather than paying full price because you suddenly realize you need the item now.

One of my clients, Lynn, worked full-time as a financial planner and shared a home office with her husband, a college professor. In addition, Lynn also stored school supplies for her children in the large sliding-door closet in her office. Inevitably, her work was constantly interrupted as she stopped to search for supplies that she or one of her family members needed for a project.

After gathering and grouping all of Lynn's supplies into clearly marked bins, we separated her business materials from the supplies used by all family members.

The left side of the closet now houses Lynn's brochures, business cards, handouts and audiotapes. The middle contains notepads, pens, tape and binders for everyone to use. Her children can come in for supplies and find things on their own without interrupting her work because all items have a home and they know where to find them.

Lynn's marketing brochures and client handouts are organized using two methods. Her most frequently accessed brochures are held in horizontal stacking trays. The remaining 20 to 30 are filed alphabetically in a portable vertical file frame. Now when she arrives from her corporate office with armfuls of new brochures and client marketing materials, she saves time by immediately filing them into her new system, which, in turn, avoids creating piles on her desk!

Being organized has also significantly reduced the amount of money this client spends buying unnecessary supplies.

She recently told me, "Between avoiding last-minute shopping trips and no longer purchasing duplicate items, I am probably saving at least $300 every year. That doesn't even take into account my time away from work when I used to run off in the middle of my day to get an urgent supply for one my kid's school projects. As a mother of two children in high school, I am still impressed by my new ability to get more accomplished in a day. A good financial planner is responsible for helping other people save money and 'stay on top of things.' My new organizing methods have increased

"Between avoiding last-minute shopping trips and no longer purchasing duplicate items, I am probably saving at least $300 every year."

my confidence. I no longer rush around in a panic or become easily distracted from my business."

Where are My Spare Ink Cartridges?

Can you find your extra ink cartridges? Do you even know if you have an extra cartridge? If you answer no to either of these questions and you are on a tight deadline, you might find yourself running frantically to the store and paying full retail.

Ink cartridges can be a high-ticket item. You will save money by purchasing your ink in advance at a discount ink outlet like www.PrintPal.com via snail mail. If you want to go green, consider buying ink refill packs. You inject new ink into your old printer cartridge. I was skeptical about this for years after hearing horror stories about ink spills and messes. So far, I am on refill #6 and have not had any problems. I save time and money and no longer have to recycle my empty ink cartridges to help the environment. I feel that I am now protecting the earth by not adding more plastic to our landfills. If you don't want to try this method, make sure to recycle your empty cartridges. Donate them to schools which use them for fundraisers, or you can send them back to the manufacturers, many of whom include free return envelopes. You can also mail them for free in the pre-labeled mailing pouches provided by your local post office, which will recycle them.

Never fear, if you are a typical client, by the time your office is organized, you will probably find the four to five missing boxes of stapler refills. This might make you feel relieved until you realize that those extra boxes probably represent at least three unnecessary trips to the office supply store.

If you suffer from these common lost but not found dilemmas, don't beat yourself up. Most people spend 55 minutes a day looking for lost items that they know they own.[13] The good news: For every hour of pre-planning and organizing, you will save three to four hours from not looking for lost items. It does pay to plan and organize where your office supplies will live.

This chapter will show you how to organize your supplies so that you can find every office supply you own in 30 seconds or less. Once you can find something in seconds, you can spend more time creating your business, making money and doing what you love.

Where to Begin?

The first step to taking charge of your supplies is exploring the deep recesses of your desk, cabinets and closets. Once your closet is empty, I will show you easy methods to keep your supplies from overtaking your workspace. You will also learn how to create areas to hold back-up supplies so they will not hinder your business at hand. Before you start, buy the organizing supplies listed on the next page.

> For every hour of pre-planning and organizing, you will save three to four hours from not looking for lost items.

Buy Supplies to Hold Your Supplies

5 Plastic shoeboxes with lids[14]

5 Doublewide plastic shoeboxes with lids

Double size shoeboxes are about the same height as regular shoeboxes but approximately 9" wide to conveniently accommodate 8.5 x 11 paper and notepads.

Ziploc baggies

1 box of each—quart and gallon size.

1. Gather: Begin your attack in the morning when you are fresh. Empty out every closet, cupboard and drawer in your office. Think about other areas throughout your home (if you have a home office) that also might contain office supplies and gather them into the office as well. This undertaking may seem daunting, but once you get started, you will build momentum and may even enjoy the process. Clearing out supplies can be surprisingly rewarding. In a customer survey conducted by Ikea, a popular furnishings store, 31% of the respondents reported that they were more satisfied after clearing out their closets than they were after sex.[15]

This project might take the best part of a day depending on your supplies situation. The more thorough you are in gathering your supplies, the more time and money you will save in the future, so be merciless. Collect all office-related items from every area of your home and office. Then spread these materials out on an empty desktop, table or floor. Doing this will allow you to see exactly what you have and what items you need, if any.

2. Group: Once your items are gathered, you may discover that you have five boxes of staples and 20 brand-new packages of Post-it notes. If this is your reality, don't feel bad; overbuying is a common phenomenon for the disorganized. One of my clients found that he owned seven boxes of staples but by the end of the day, we still could not find the stapler. Another client found over 50 pads of Post-it notepads. Group your items, like with like. What this means is place all paper with paper, pens with pens and pencils with pencils. This is where plastic containers and baggies come in handy—simply toss items into bins and bags as you find them.

3. Categorize: Once items are grouped, the next step is to merge into categories by purpose. Choose categories that are related to a single task, such as "things that stick" (one of my favorite fun category names). This category might include your scotch tape, masking tape, glue, sticky tack and so on.

Choose categories that are related to a single task, such as "things that stick."

4. Eliminate: Once you have grouped your items into categories, you will begin to get a clear picture of just how many supplies you own. This is the perfect time to take stock, make choices and eliminate the excess. In general, don't keep more than three extras of a given item. A good rule of thumb is to keep the amount of supplies you will use throughout the course of one year. Even if you live in the Taj Mahal, you don't need to exert the energy and effort it takes to track and maintain roomfuls of supplies. Conserve your energy for more important matters and limit your bevy to a one-year supply.

add space TIPS

Consider donating your excess supplies to a local school. Teachers often use their personal money to buy paper and pencils and other supplies for students without the means to buy their own. They also sometimes raise money recycling ink cartridges. Your contribution will be put to good use and greatly appreciated.

5. Containerize: Once you have sorted, grouped, categorized and eliminated, you can containerize, placing your categorized, groups of items into containers. Label these containers with their broad categories—Things that Stick, etc. Plastic shoeboxes with lids make excellent storage devices for loose office supplies. Having lids on your boxes helps you stack them together on shelves.

Printer paper and paper pads fit perfectly into the double-sized shoeboxes.

Useful Container Titles

Things that Stick

Things that Bind

Things that Write

Post-it notes and Notepads

Loose Paper

CDs and Cases

6. Label: Make sure that you label your containers with category names that make it easy for you to remember what is inside. Choose the name you are most likely to think of first when you go to look for an item. For instance, a box containing staples and paperclips could be labeled "Things that Bind", or simply, "Staples/Paperclips."

Label machines are handy and cost-effective but are not essential for this process. You can also use computer adhesive labels or write on the sticky side of a Post-it note and adhere it to the inside of your clear box with the writing showing out.

addSpace TIPS

If you decide to buy a label machine, compare prices of the refill tape along with the price of the machine. A less expensive label maker may seem like a better deal, but the cost of the refill tape may be higher than for a more expensive machine, making it less of a bargain over time.

It is helpful to print two labels and put one on both the short and long end of each box. This way, if you shift your supplies in another direction on the shelf later on, your labels will still show.

Store for Quick Retrieval

Once you have consolidated and containerized, you will want to create an office supplies space where you can store all your back-up office supplies.

A closet outfitted with floor-to-ceiling shelves is the ideal storage area for your supplies. If you don't have a closet, however, you can use a free-standing bookshelf. If you don't like visual clutter, consider covering the cabinets with doors or with a curtain.

Whatever kind of storage you choose, the most important task will be to keep *all* your extra supplies in this area. This makes it clear to you and everyone else using the office where to go to quickly find any supply.

With this exercise complete, you will be able to

find any supply within 30 seconds. No more wasted time and money looking for lost items or shopping for duplicates!

addSpace Action Steps

1. Gather all supplies into one space.
2. Group them together.
3. Separate into categories.
4. Eliminate duplicates.
5. Containerize to optimize storage space.
6. Label containers for easy retrieval.

Voilà!

You have the knowledge and tools to master the art of containing and consolidating your office supplies. Even if your office space is small, you still need to delegate part of your space for supplies if you want to stop wasting time on the search. Whatever you do, try to avoid buying your supplies from a warehouse store. The price might be better until you factor in the cost and energy required to store and maintain control over your collection until it is diminished.

If you frequently have gooey products to store, consider using plastic containers. This way, the goop will stay in the container in the event of a leak.

For massive CD collections, consider removing the jewel cases and storing your CDs in a three-ring binder. Make sure to use alphabetical divider pages within your three-ring binder. This way, you can move the headings as your collection expands and you add more pages.

Almost every office has at least a double shoebox full of electrical cords and wires. Try to keep this collection within one box. A good rule of thumb for your cords: If you have never used the cord and it is still wrapped in its original plastic bag or twist-tie, all of the equipment it came with works without it now, it has been over one year, and you are not setting up a new office, you can probably let it go.

If you have never used the cord and it is still wrapped in its original plastic bag or twist-tie, all of the equipment it came with works without it . . . you can probably let it go.

Chapter Three

· ·

Mastering Your
Home Office

"There is no one-way to do anything. It is all about you and how you think and react to outside stimulus."

Read This Chapter First If You Resonate With These Questions:

Do you have to get up from your desk chair to get to your file drawers?

. . . .

Can you reach your extra printer paper without standing?

. . . .

Do your file drawers go to battle when you try to open them?

Just like a well-designed kitchen, an optimized and well-equipped office will have all tools within arm's reach of the main work area. It pays to take the time to organize your office space. A study conducted by a Boston marketing firm reports that Americans waste over 12 weeks a year looking for lost items they know they have but can't find.[16]

Here is a little bit of trivia to help get you motivated: The time it takes a corporate employee to return to

their desk after leaving for a supply is 7.2 minutes. The average time it takes for a home-based businessperson to return is 17 minutes! After all, the dog wants some attention, the dryer needs loading and a snack calls out to us from the kitchen. These are a few of the hazards of working in a home office.

Office Organization

The minimum furniture requirement needed in a home-based office is a desk, chair, file drawer and cabinet or shelf. A computer, printer, phone, and scheduling device are the items that will round out a well-equipped office.

Your desk can be a large table (think dining size) or an actual office desk. Small folding tables are too restrictive and won't hold your computer plus other necessary paperwork. Check your local thrift store for office furniture if you need to save money as you start your business. The best desk set-up leaves 60% of the flat area empty. This is why you need a large surface.

The ultimate desk for most businesses will have an L-shaped configuration. With computers, phones and printers, an L allows you to position your computer monitor in the corner and your work to flow on either side. If you have a hard drive tower, it should be placed below the desk, not on the desktop. The side facing the door should provide the most spacious surface with the least amount of collateral items, possibly only a phone beside the monitor. If you have frequent visitors, position a guest chair on the opposite side of this section of the desk. The other side of the L can hold your papers in progress (your Action files) using the vertical, stepped file holder described in the "Master Your Papers!" chapter. If you do not have a shelf to hold your printer above or below the desktop, move it to a side table or file cabinet within arm's reach.

An ergonomically designed desk chair is worth more than the money you invest. Your old dining room chair will bring quick fatigue and leave your back tweaked at the end of the day. You might also want to elevate your monitor and check into ergonomic wrist and footrests if you spend over six hours a day at your desk.

An ergonomically designed desk chair is worth more than the money you invest.

File Cabinets

File drawers will protect your desk from overflowing paperwork. Many of my clients have tried to use "pretty" or decorative file baskets for their paperwork. File boxes pose several hazards: You pile things on top because you don't take the time to remove the lid so that you can actually file. Sound familiar? They also tend to fall apart and don't have rails for hanging file folders. If you can't or don't use hanging files, your folders fall down and slip around, making it impossible to retrieve files without a time-consuming investigation. I could give you at least 20 more reasons to use proper file cabinets but will illustrate this point with a few case studies.

A successful photographer operated her business in a converted garage office. When we began working together, there were piles of papers, prints, cards and film negatives spread across every surface of her office and also piled onto the floor. There were over 20 different file boxes, baskets and bins, all overflowing with papers. As we uncovered each box and delved inside, we discovered that some had more papers stacked on top than inside. Others were full, but the papers within had fallen into piles or were in unmarked manila folders.

By the time all of Mia's papers were purged and organized, we had discarded over eight trash bags of paper. We also uncovered eight different filing systems that she had started to create in the course of her 10 years in business. She was entirely amazed to discover that she had developed so many systems and did not use any. You see, it wasn't that she had never tried to get organized. Mia had simply not created a sustainable system because she kept getting caught up in "pretty" versus functional systems. She did not treat her business as a business. The decorative file bins were easier on the eyes than practical places to file. In the end, Mia purchased two lateral file cabinets to organize her eight drawers of papers and negatives. She made them visually acceptable by covering them with table runners, framed prints, cards and crystals. There are many ways to create a beautiful office without sacrificing functionality.

Another writer client, Libby, begged me not to make her use file cabinets. She felt very strongly that once her files were in a drawer, they would be forgotten forever. As a visual learner, Libby was inspired to write when she had her files in sight. Luckily, she had retrofitted her large sliding two-door closet with floor-to-ceiling shelves. I was able to create a visual file system by using 16 vertical, stepped file holders.[17] Each holder provided slots for eight files. With four holders placed side by side on each shelf, and four shelves available, she had 128 folders, all within sight of her desk chair. Each file was clearly titled and segmented by subject. Libby's productivity soared once her papers were organized and visually inspirational!

Whatever tools you choose, I highly recommend treating your business like a business. Buy business caliber tools. A real file cabinet will serve you for years. If you want to save money, thrift stores often sell high-quality cabinets for $15 to $30, as opposed to the $120 cabinet at the office supply store. Make sure that the file

Whatever tools you choose, I highly recommend treating your business like a business. Buy business caliber tools. A real file cabinet will serve you for years.

cabinet you purchase has drawers with sliding tracks and wheels and, if possible, built-in side rails to hold your hanging files. Drawers manufactured with industrial strength side rails are always easier to use than the rail kits you buy and assemble to fit within the drawers. There is nothing worse than battling with jammed or faulty file drawers when you are trying to work. Many file systems falter simply because the drawers are too hard to open and people get tired of the fight.

Electronics

Whatever your business, a computer loaded with the proper programs will save you countless hours of frustration and wasted time. As I am sure you know, computers also allow you to send and receive emails and faxes and to access the Internet.

If you are not completely computer savvy, now is the time to jump in and learn. Many computer courses are available, including the free courses at the public library or local community center. Community colleges and adult education programs are other good resources. Check the Internet for free computer training class schedules. You could also learn by being tutored one-on-one by a neighbor or business colleague. Learning computer basics is a mandatory investment for your future.

A printer will help you prepare documents to give to your clients or print reference materials for your projects. Many printers now scan, copy, fax and print. Hewlett Packard all-in-one models are a cost-effective solution for start-up businesses.

Keep Business Separate From Personal

I had a very talented client, Sue, who operated a home-based business and also took care of all of the family bills within the same office space. When we first met, she could not decide which activities to prioritize, and her business was suffering. She was easily influenced by visual clutter and caught up in inertia, unable to focus on any one thing.

Everything in Sue's life was overdue. She did not know whether to spend her energy on home or work tasks. She would begin paying her personal bills and the business line would ring. Bills were shoved aside as she scrambled to take notes, and then when she hung up the phone, she didn't know what to do next. Maybe go back to paying bills? But where did they go? Sound familiar? This is why everyone needs to keep their personal papers separated from work papers, no matter how left-brained they are.

Work projects combined with bills and personal correspondence can create a very messy environment.

After interviewing Sue, I decided to completely separate her business and personal workspace and actually set up two workstations in her home. Her home office was now the sole proprietor of her business. A small desk in the kitchen became the home base for personal bills and files. She has a real physical boundary between work and her personal tasks. Now that she has to physically get up and move to switch out of business mode, her productivity and concentration have increased dramatically.

addSpace **TIPS** If you must keep personal paperwork in your business office, keep them separated in file drawers and also in the vertical action files on your desktop. Use the same filing protocol to keep it simple, but always keep these papers physically separated.

Everyone's work habits and thought processes vary. This particular client was easily sidetracked. It benefited her to completely separate personal and business: other folks might find that simply keeping these papers separated on the desk and in file drawers will do the trick. Again, there is no one-way to do anything. It is all about *you* and how you think and react to outside stimulus.

If you are also in charge of your personal finances and find it hard to remain focused on one task at a time, you might want to create a separate desk space or counter area for your personal finances. Designate a corner of your kitchen counter for bills and personal correspondence.

Keeping personal affairs out the office will help you focus on work when you are in your office. Storing your personal papers away from your business space also helps make your home office eligible for a complete tax write-off each year.

If you need to have both personal and business papers in the same room, keep them physically separated. Think left and right separation. In my experience, top and bottom does not seem to be as effective. Some people have the ability to keep personal and business papers in the same workspace. If this is the case, I would definitely recommend an L-shaped desk configuration with personal papers to the left of the monitor and business to the right. If you try this and find you are becoming easily sidetracked with personal projects, set up another desk for your personal correspondence, perhaps behind your main workstation so it is not directly in your line of sight.

Now that you have learned the basic skills of organizing your desk and office, you are ready to move on to making those pesky piles of business cards you have collected over the years work for you!

There is no one-way to do anything. It is all about you and how you think and react to outside stimulus.

addSpace Action Steps

1. Make sure you are using business caliber tools in your office.
2. Invest in file cabinets that open easily and have built-in rails for hanging files.
3. Design an L-shaped desk configuration.
4. Separate your personal and business papers.

In the next chapter, you will discover how to get those piles of business cards off of your desk and turn them into useable information. You will also learn how to keep your important business contacts in close reach and how to develop a masterful follow-up system to increase your business success.

Chapter Four

Business Contacts
Mastery

" Managing your contact list and business card collection will put you a step closer to truly being in control of your business. "

Read This Chapter First if You Resonate With These Questions:

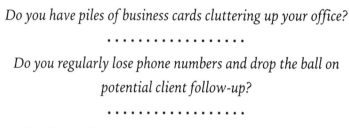

Do you have piles of business cards cluttering up your office?

· · · · · · · · · · · · · · · ·

Do you regularly lose phone numbers and drop the ball on potential client follow-up?

· · · · · · · · · · · · · · · ·

Would you like to appear more professional and keep in touch with your existing clients on a regular basis?

Most offices that I am called in to help with have at least one pile of business cards strategically positioned by the phone for future reference. Sometimes these neat little piles are grouped into multiple stacks, which become scattered as they topple off their original stacks. Sadly, even before toppling, this method usually fails when quick access to specific names or numbers is critical. We typically waste eight hours per week trying to find documents we need, and piling isn't an effective approach.[18]

Sam was an entrepreneurial client who had piles and piles of business card contacts spread throughout his office. Before we began streamlining his office, the method he used to organize this potential new business was to keep them rubber banded into categories. A big challenge often arose when someone left a voice mail and did not leave his or her phone number.

Sam could not put his finger on the relevant information when he needed to return the call. He literally had to sort through a pile of 50+ cards to find the information. Although it was obvious that he was making a big effort to get organized, his method did not serve him. Instead of investing the time upfront to manage and input his contacts, he was spending excessive time and energy trying to keep his cards banded together into groups. Frustrated and harried, Sam had barely enough time or energy to do his actual business while he was chasing names, numbers and important details.

I want to help you eliminate those piles of business cards that you frequently collect while networking. I also want you to find your business contacts and email addresses effortlessly the moment that you need them. This chapter contains easy and proven methods that my clients use regularly to connect with influential contacts and prospective clients by using a computer reminder system.

When you use the power of current technology, it doesn't take long to streamline your business contact information into a workable database. Your vital contact information becomes only a keyboard stroke away.

What Happened to That Phone Number?

At the most fundamental level, every company has customers, and every company should maintain some basic information about those customers (names, addresses, purchases, contracts, invoices, etc.). According to an article published by the American Marketing Association, any company that wants to spend more time servicing clients than recruiting customers should have some basic "Contact Relationship Management Technology" (CRM) to track and serve their customers.[19]

The most important key to customer and prospect follow-up is to keep all of your contact information within a single database. Computer programs like ACT, Outlook, Goldmine or Entourage will organize and prioritize your influential names and numbers. If you don't have a contact management program, you can also use your email database or create a spreadsheet in Excel.

With most CRM programs, you can enter and store all business cards and potential client names in one

When you use the power of current technology, it doesn't take long to streamline your business contact information into a workable database.

database, then, most importantly, schedule follow-up calls to secure new business!

This method is incredibly liberating for those of us with an entrepreneurial or artistic temperament. Most artists (and actually most folks in general) hate to sell. When information is harnessed, hardcore sales can take a back seat to follow-up that honors verbal promises.

The best CRM programs will allow you to view your emails through that same program. With ACT, Outlook and Entourage, you will have all past history and email correspondence linked right to each specific business contact. These programs will organize your telephone book of contacts and clients and improve your time management capabilities through their appointment calendar and "to do" list tasks that show you exactly what needs to be done today. You will begin to follow up when you say you will and increase your perceived level of professionalism.

An artist client of mine is a very talented networker. Jessie loves meeting new people and finding common interests. This put her two steps ahead as she markets her graphic design services. Before getting organized, her downfall was that, although she made great connections and collected numerous business cards, she failed to follow up. She did not take time after these events to input her new contacts into a database or schedule the reminders to reconnect as promised. Jessie spent a lot of time meeting people, but it was time wasted because she never remembered whom she needed to call or when! Although people really enjoyed meeting her, they were left with a less than professional impression.

Can you imagine what they thought of Jessie when she didn't follow up as promised? They would probably hesitate to give her work because they might worry that their project might also fall through the cracks.

Take the Time to Save Your Time

Take the time to input your business leads into a proper contact management program. Whatever program you choose, it pays to make the right database choice in the beginning. A contact management system will help you take control of your business and become proactive with its growth patterns.

Choose a contact management system that will grow with your company, morph with various tasks and have the ability to export or upgrade as technology improves.

You also want to choose a CRM program that syncs with your other business tools. For those of us who still use paper calendars, the choice is less complicated. For those who use electronic scheduling devices, the choices become more critical.

I choose to keep my schedule and daily "to-dos" on paper, but I'm also able to reap the benefits of my computer database. As I collect business contacts, I input them into Entourage, the Macintosh equivalent of Outlook. I pencil short-term follow-up calls and appointments immediately into my book. For long-term and repeat follow-up protocols, I use the reminder system built into Entourage, which is also linked to my email program. When the time arrives for a follow-up, my email program reminds me.

Some clients use Excel to store their contacts. The one distinct disadvantage of this program is that it cannot be synched with a calendar or scheduling program. This means that when you are cued from your calendar to follow up with a contact, you have to move to another program to find their number or other relevant information.

Contact management programs usually cost between $100 and $2,000 dollars. The best place to find the one that works for you is on the Internet. It is easy to download these programs and try them before you buy them. Another type of contact manager is a PIM, (personal information manager). They are less expensive but lack many of the features mentioned in this chapter. You should get a program that will grow with your needs. Life is certainly getting more complicated, but a good contact management program will simplify your life and make you feel like you're organized and really in control.

Researching and implementing the right system from the beginning will pay off in long-term profits. As Abe Lincoln said, "One hour of preparation saves me eight hours of perspiration." Consider your specific business needs and consider every option available. Ask associates within your industry what they use and how it works for them. After this research, you will be able to determine which program will serve you best.

When Was I Supposed to Follow Up?

Managing your contact list and business card collection will put you a step closer to truly being in control of your business. Have you ever asked yourself, "When did I promise to follow up?" as you were looking at somebody's card? Each time you return from a networking event or meeting, schedule time to enter the information into your database.

It's time to join the twenty-first century. Customer Relationship Management software (CRM) offers so many advantages over paper systems. It keeps you from missing important meetings and appointments. It reminds you of important follow-up calls and tasks.

With any good CRM program, you can input and

Managing your contact list and business card collection will put you a step closer to truly being in control of your business.

store all business card information into one database. The quick access to contact information eliminates wasted time, no matter where you happen to be. You'll love it the first time you find yourself in need of someone's number or address, and you remember it's right there in your cell phone because you keep it synchronized to your computer. CRM systems help you track your income opportunities and provide powerful reports for managing the growth of your business.

Once you have your contacts stored safely into one database, you can begin to create your company follow-through protocol. For this task, you will need to set up a calendar reminder system. This empowers you to schedule follow-up calls with potential clients and create more new business.

If you are a new business owner, you will probably spend 80% of your time marketing your services or product, and only 20% performing the actual work that you market. This is why managing all of your potential client information is vital.

---

addSpace TIPS If you attend a conference or seminar, block time the next day to revisit the information you gleaned and update your database with your new business contacts. It is important to block time immediately after the event to revisit that information. If you cannot block time within 24 hours to assimilate the information, consider skipping the event.

Here Is a Quicker Method

It pays to invest in a good business card scanner. A good card scanner will import the information into your database as quick as you can collect the business card. As you scan, you will have the option to add additional phone numbers and notes about each contact. Simply scan and import each card into your database, categorize them appropriately and schedule important reminders to reconnect.

Scanning your business cards will alleviate the piles of cards cluttering your desk. Scan cards once a week and always immediately after each networking event to ensure that your follow-up is timely and effective. Your bottom line will increase as you fine-tune your data entry and optimize your office technology.

If you dread inputting data or scanning your business leads, hire a high school or college student to perform this task for you—but only after learning to do it yourself. Make sure to spot-check their work for accuracy.

Don't Forget to Schedule Your Follow-Ups

The most effective way to schedule follow-up calls and meetings is to do it when you input the new contact into your contact management program.

Take the time to develop follow-up protocol that

If you are a new business owner, you will probably spend 80% of your time marketing your services or product, and only 20% performing the actual work that you market.

is relevant to your business model. You can preset reminder protocols and save them for new contacts as they become part of your database.

For instance, when you first meet someone at a networking event, how often and how soon do you want to follow up? You will use your generic protocol for most leads. If contacting once a month is appropriate, when you import that name, schedule the monthly follow-up reminder protocol at the same time. Follow this protocol and your schedule will be maintained with ease and joy. Your bottomline finances will increase along with your level of professionalism.

Maybe you have a few hot leads that require immediate attention and you don't want to forget to call. As they are imported, schedule a priority follow-up protocol with their name.

Most contact management programs are under-utilized. On average, end users tap only 20% of the program's capability. As I mention in the Masters Hire Other Masters chapter, it pays to take a class in your CRM program or hire a tutor from the very beginning. Your bottomline cash results will more than pay for the time and money spent learning to set follow-up reminders and import data.

Follow this protocol and your schedule will be maintained with ease and joy. Your bottomline finances will increase along with your level of professionalism.

1. Decide which contact management program and scheduling device you will use.

2. Take a class, hire a tutor or enlist a business associate to teach you the program.

3. Invest in a business card scanner.

4. Learn to import business cards with a scanner to quickly input new contacts into your database. Subcontract this task after you know how to do it yourself.

5. Construct follow-up protocol relevant to your particular industry.

It's time to look at ways to expedite your business success and master your inbox. In the next chapter, you will learn how to avoid the deep vortex of email oblivion.

• Notes •

Chapter Five

Become the
Master
of Your Inbox

"One of the most common reasons that people have clutter in their lives is the lack of decision-making. Your inbox is no exception to this rule."

Read This Chapter First If You Resonate With These Questions:

Do emails entice you to interrupt your workflow more than three times a day?

. . . .

Do you feel controlled by your inbox?

. . . .

Do you spend more than half an hour sorting through junk mail on a daily basis?

Technology can be a blessing in disguise. It brings information to us at an amazing pace. At the same time, it forces us to react at faster and faster speeds. Once our computer is turned on and open for business, emails consistently force their way into our day. We need solid discipline and new skill sets to keep this potentially fabulous piece of technology from becoming our dictator.

You can become the master of your inbox. You can

also learn how to apply simple rules to maintain proper email etiquette. When you apply a few of these simple and powerful techniques, you will shave hours off of your email correspondence.

How Can I Control This Beast?

A home-based business client, Maggie, candidly admitted to me that once she started checking her emails, she frequently became glued to her inbox for hours. My suggestion was that she check her emails only twice a day, once in the morning just before she picked up her kids from pre-school and once in the afternoon just before they awoke from their nap. By partitioning this task into a tight timeframe, Maggie automatically had to quit in order to begin her next pressing task, which in her case was attending to her children.

You might not have kids, but you probably have tasks that need to be performed at predetermined times. When you first begin learning how to control your email habits, it helps to use tasks to define the parameters around when you will check your inbox.

An interesting email from a client, Kyla, arrived to my inbox as I was writing this chapter. This is what she said: "I made another 'discovery' yesterday . . . well, actually my supervisor did. I've had this habit of compulsively checking emails, keeping Outlook open all

You *can* become the master of your inbox.

day. I didn't realize how much I was emailing until he told me he'd received about 40 emails from me spaced at random times throughout the day. Yikes! I know I've read that you should only check it a few times a day, and now I have motivation to do so. There's never been a complaint about my productivity (at this job!), but I think, how much more I could get done with more focus."

Kyla is not alone. Even way back in 2003, the average worker sent and received over 190 messages each day![20] In August 2008, the estimated number of emails sent per day worldwide was around 210 billion.[21]

Everyone should aspire to check their emails only two times a day, three times max, and always during predetermined times.

As our inbox grows, it also becomes incredibly valuable to know how to craft rules to keep spam solicitations out and useful correspondence filed into proper folders. This chapter will show you little tricks to start mastering your inbox instead of allowing it to control you!

Forget About It!

Okay, so I know what you are thinking, there is no way that you can only check your emails two to three times a day. "What if I lose business? When clients want

Start your morning by not checking your emails or voicemails. Instead, use the first hour of your day to plan that day.

answers, they want answers." Trust me, I hear these comments constantly from clients. It is true that you can be a successful businessperson and only check emails two to three times a day, even if you are a mortgage banker or financial consultant. Consider Timothy Ferriss, author of *The 4-Hour Workweek*. He only checks his inbox once a week and he is one of the New Rich! He is proof that you can become insanely successful without also becoming a slave to your technology.

Here's what to do. Start your morning by *not* checking your emails or voicemails. Instead, use the first hour of your day to plan that day. Get organized and determine your priority tasks. Look at your scheduled activities and list the "to do's" for that day *before* you check your inbox or listen to your voicemail. Only after you have completed this step should you check emails and phone messages.

An attendee of one of my time management seminars voiced his opinion when I covered this segment. He said, "Well, my industry is an exception because sometimes when we get into the office, the first message we receive in an email or on voicemail is that a client has died. This is really important news." Not wanting to make light of this comment, I couldn't help but quickly reply, "Will he be any more dead if you respond an hour later? What will happen to this client if you take the time to organize your day before reacting to this news?"

My point is this—everything can wait at least an hour. If you normally get into the office at 8 am, spend one hour planning. Wait until 9 am to begin contacting clients and reacting to their needs. If your industry demands that you begin interacting with clients at 8 am, I guarantee that you will work fewer hours, get more accomplished and have exceptionally less stress if you arrive at 7 am to plan your day.

Planning Versus Reacting

Why is it important to plan your day before you check your inbox? Because when you finally do check emails and get barraged by requests for information and other tasks, you will know how and when you can respond based on your overall goals for the day.

It is true that once you read your emails, an important email request might suddenly take priority for the day. However, the huge difference is this: After planning your day, when you do decide to react to the email and make it a priority task, you will know exactly what you will have to place on the back burner to accomplish it. You will also know exactly why you have decided to make this task your new priority.

Remember, when you begin your day with email correspondence, you can potentially get stuck for hours

After planning your day, when you do decide to react to the email and make it a priority task, you will know exactly what you will have to place on the back burner to accomplish it.

and lose total focus from the real work intended for that day.

If you plan your day and have goals in place before you open your inbox, you will easily see which emails fall into that day's work. You can also easily decide what you can put off until later or even the next day— AFTER your goals are completed.

Keep a Tight Timeline

If you must check your emails three times a day, do the midday check just before lunch. This way, you will be motivated to get offline to eat and won't spend too much time dallying over unimportant items. If you frequently forget to eat, schedule an alarm clock to remind you to get up, get out of your seat and nourish your body. Please try to eat away from your desk. Studies show that adequate nourishment for workers can raise productivity levels by 20%.[22]

If you are a "two checks a day" person, the second time to visit your inbox should be towards the end of each day. Do this about one hour before you finish for the day and you will have time to respond to the quick requests.

You can also plan who will receive your attention the following morning during your planning time.

As a regular "circular" routine, the next morning you start by planning, respond to emails from the previous day and then move on to the new correspondence.

It takes self-discipline to master this strategy but the rewards are huge. You will be able to keep your focus and take your business to the next level.

No one expects instant response from their email, and if they do, simply inform them of your new practice the next time you respond. You might create a signature line similar to this, "In an effort to serve my clients more effectively, I am focusing on the business at hand and checking emails twice a day. I will get back with you within 24 hours. If this is an emergency request and cannot wait, please contact me at 333.333.3333."

No one expects instant response from their email, and if they do, simply inform them of your new practice the next time you respond.

Read It, Act on It and Be Done With It!

One of the most common reasons that people have clutter in their lives is the lack of decision-making. Your inbox is no exception to this rule. One of my clients, Seth, had over 2,850 emails in his inbox when we began working together. He felt overwhelmed, and rightfully so, and he had no idea where to begin. It was all a jumble in his mind and he hated this piece of technology. It affected his life so dramatically that he spent sleepless nights worrying if he had overlooked an important business detail that had arrived in the form of an email.

One of the reasons why I suggest that you carve out specific niches of time throughout the day to read your emails is so that this will not happen to you. When you have time set aside to deal with emails, you will also have time to do what I will now suggest.

Read it, act on it and move on. This literally means that when you read an email, make a decision right then and there what you are going to do about it. Will you respond? Flag it as an action item? Move it to another folder or delete? These are your basic choices.

If you want to be effective, you will learn to make quick decisions about each email that you read, respond quickly or forward it without letting it sit in your inbox.

When an email requires a quick response, do it right away and then delete. If it requires more time than you have allotted in your schedule at the moment, flag it as an upcoming task and place it within one of your action categories, as explained in Chapter One.

When you receive numerous emails from the same person or regarding the same subject that you can't delete and need to save, create a folder and move those items into it. If they arrive frequently, write a rule that will automatically push these emails into a predetermined

> Read it, act on it and move on. This literally means that when you read an email, make a decision right then and there what you are going to do about it.

folder within your inbox. This way, when you are ready to work on that topic, everything is in one neat folder. You can then take action on all related items at the same time which, in turn, will save you hours.

Learn to Write Rules and Create Signatures

Did you know that you can place filters on any message that arrives into your inbox? You can also set up a system to automatically move specific client emails into project folders.

You can write rules based on the subject line or the sender or both. Get creative and keep your inbox folder headings fairly generic. For instance, Seth received numerous emails from his employees regarding ongoing projects. Once we created an email rule for these employees, their emails were moved into separate project folders as they arrived to his inbox. When he set aside time to focus on a specific project, he simply opened that email folder to see what action was needed from him and what each employee was doing regarding that project.

As a result, more than a third of his emails then became recognizable as non-urgent because they were not project-oriented. After we wrote more rules, his daily reading was reduced to less than 100 total emails per day.

Email programs vary, but almost all of them give you tools to filter unwanted emails. Start learning these tricks by checking in the Tools menu on your navigation bar while your email program is open. There should be a choice titled "write rules" or something similar. You have many choices when it comes to email rules. Do you want to banish this address forever into your junk mail file or simply have it automatically moved to a client project folder that you can check later when you are working on their job?

Save Drafts of Frequently Repeated Email Subjects

If you find yourself creating the same email response over and over again, save it in your drafts folder for future responses. For instance, an author client receives numerous requests for her speaking "one sheet." It is posted on her website, but she wants to respond personally to these requests to further build her relationships.

To achieve this goal and save time, Kay created a very personal email response, attaching her "one sheet," with a link to her website. She then saved this email as a draft with "Speaker Information" in the subject line.

When she receives requests for this type of information, Kay simply pulls up the draft, personalizes it with the new recipient name, adds anther sentence to make it truly unique and forwards it to the recipient.

---

add Space
TIPS If you send a draft, make sure to delete all forwarding notes in your email before you resend your draft. It typically appears in the subject line and at the end of the email and looks like this *FW*: or *Forwarded Message* or—*End of Forwarded Message*

Automatically Personalize Your Email Sign Offs

Have you set up a personalized email signature? Email signatures should include your name, title, business name and phone and fax numbers. They might also include your tagline, logo or photo. Create a business signature and set it to automatically appear on emails that you send. This will save you time and help with your marketing efforts. You never know when your email might be forwarded, and it pays to attach the correct contact information for you and your company!

You can create and save other email signatures to use with different types of clients or for personal emails. Make sure to double-check and choose an alternative signature, if necessary, before you hit Send.

Everyone has a friend (or friend of a friend) who

is an expert emailer. Find that person and enlist their aid. Ask them to give you a personalized tour of your email program capabilities. Pay them, if you have to, or sign up for a class at your local college. Take the time to master your technology! It will be well worth the money and time investment.

Please respond to important emails to let the person know that you have received their correspondence.

A Word About Email Etiquette

Please respond to important emails to let the person know that you have received their correspondence. This does not mean that you need to write a lengthy response or shove aside your current project to meet their request. If you decide not to take action immediately, simply reply with, "I have received your email and will get back with you as soon as possible." This response could also be saved as a draft for future email responses.

addSpace Email Action Steps

1. **Determine** which two to three times a day are the best to check your emails and adhere rigidly to that schedule for at least one week. Watch how your productivity soars! Remember that it takes three to four weeks of solid practice to develop a new habit.

2. **Set up** an autoresponse signature that includes your name, title, company, web address and phone number to automatically appear in your outbound emails.

3. **Learn how** to write rules in your email program and control the amount of junk you have to sort through every day.

4. **Create drafts** for frequent recurring email responses. Now that you know how to control your urges to check your email 25 times per day, you are ready to move on to learning how to say no and protecting your schedule from spur-of-the-moment interlopers! Did you hear someone scream fire?!

Remember that it takes three to four weeks of solid practice to develop a new habit.

• Notes •

Chapter Six

How to Let Go
and Master Your
Schedule

"One of the most
important tools
for an organized
businessperson is a
proper scheduling
device."

Read This Chapter First if You Resonate With These Questions:

*Have your day-to-day activities taken over
every hour in your life?*

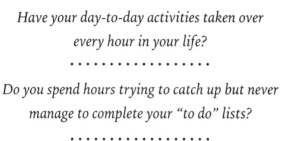

*Do you spend hours trying to catch up but never
manage to complete your "to do" lists?*

Are you frequently late for meetings?

Time is a finite resource. Everyone has the same amount of hours in the day and the same amount of days in the week. When your schedule is overbooked, the result is often subtle. Minutes and hours evaporate each day from your business. You might be reading this chapter because you want to be one of the smart, successful business owners who doesn't have to work 60 to 80 hours every week to reach their goals.

It *is* possible to achieve success in a 40-hour

workweek. The first step is learning to recognize and remove the unproductive tasks from your agenda. You do have the ability to take control of your time. You will become the master of your schedule once you know that everything on your agenda is there because you choose it to be.

When you eliminate the unnecessary tasks in your life, you will be able to use your precious time to attract clients and market your services or products.

Thomas Edison said it best, "Being busy does not always mean real work. The object of all work is production or accomplishment, and to either of these ends there must be forethought, system, planning, intelligence and honest purpose as well as perspiration. Seeming to do is not doing."

As you let go of all that does not serve you, you will absolutely become more successful in less time.

Time Management
Umbrella Your Day™

You can save countless hours by grouping related tasks together into the same timeframe;[23] for instance, making all of your follow-up calls together or researching for long, uninterrupted blocks of time. To umbrella your tasks, you first need to list the recurring tasks that you perform weekly on a sheet of paper. Then you can begin to allocate time in your schedule for these recurring tasks.

> *Block tasks into similar types of activities; for instance, phone calls, paperwork, outside meetings. Divide your main job activities into five days:*
> - Planning day (Friday or Monday is optimum) Set goals/intentions, line up the week.
> - Current large project.
> - Outside appointments, client meetings.
> - Client follow-up and research.
> - Administrative, reports & paperwork.

Create specific days and chunks of time for related activities. If you need to research client files every week, schedule your research for the same day each week. The benefit of this is that when a client calls for information, you can safely tell them that you will be working on it on a specific day. I know you are thinking at this point, *But they want it now!* Trust me when I say this, clients care more about the quality of your work and whether you meet your promised delivery date more than they care about instant gratification. Quality work takes time.

As an entrepreneur for the past twenty years, I have

Clients care more about the quality of your work and whether you meet your promised delivery date more than they care about instant gratification.

learned this from my clients over and over again. You can offer price, service or quality—choose only two because you can never offer all three consistently. I have always chosen service and quality. Lower pricing always involves speed because of lower margins, which, in turn, sacrifices quality and service. Okay, enough Sales 101 training . . . The same rule applies for outside meetings, filing and phone calls. Choose two goals for each of these events and you can achieve success in any of these situations.

If you know when you are scheduled to make phone calls, you can easily tell your clients when you will be getting back to them. Filing on a regular basis will relieve you of the paper maladies that can also block your productivity.

What's Important and What's Not?

Matt was a dot.com entrepreneur client with a very busy life. He developed a booming non-profit Internet business that aligned with his passions after he had, in theory, retired. This project was so multifaceted that it was hard to decide where to spend his energies. Should he spend time developing products, searching for team players, developing partner relationships? All of these tasks demanded attention, and some had pressing deadlines.

As we began to define Matt's vision for the company and the projects that were currently in progress, it became clear what we needed to do. After listing the weekly tasks that he needed to perform to keep his company moving forward, I decided to "umbrella" each day of the week with a specific type of task.

For instance, Monday was his planning day. During that day, he would spend the morning determining his priorities for that week and developing his schedule. In the afternoon, Matt would meet with his assistant to go over his schedule and keep his schedule within the time management parameters we had developed. This planning day gave him increased clarity about which projects and tasks he could pass on to others in his corporation. With uninterrupted planning time, he was less likely to react and do it all on his own. He had the time to consider if someone else could handle it.

Successful entrepreneurs delegate as many tasks as possible to others so that they can focus on the tasks that only *they* can do and that they enjoy. This skill takes time to develop because it involves letting go of the details and focusing on the big picture. It also involves trusting others to do the task without dropping the ball.

Tuesday was his outside meeting day. Whenever possible, any and all appointments, lunches, etc. were scheduled on this day. He had a regular standing appointment out of the office on Tuesdays, so it made sense to schedule other outside meetings on that day.

Wednesday became his web development and staff meeting day. If he needed to meet with his webmaster or department heads, these appointments were scheduled for that day. Thursday was the day we set aside for his most urgent full-focus projects. This day he was to spend uninterrupted blocks of time for whatever projects that only he could do. As author Ted Johns states in his book, *Perfect Time Management*, "The damage caused to your time management by any given interruption is always twice as long as the actual duration of the interruption itself."[24] Everyone needs uninterrupted periods of time for creativity. According to Jim Miller, General Manager for US West, it takes a person 20 to 30 minutes to transition into deep, critical and creative thought.[25] Friday was designated as another inside office and planning/organizing day.

By setting up Matt's schedule with the overall intentions for each day, it became easier to eliminate the other busy tasks that did not fall under that day's heading. Amazingly, some of those busy tasks never came back. The ones that remained were moved to the day where similar tasks were done. This provided greater efficiency to Matt's workweek.

> How do you know what to eliminate? Begin by listing every task that you must accomplish in order to be successful in business.

Most clients have four to five major tasks that they must do regularly in order to succeed. Examples might be: phone calls, client presentations, email promotions, Internet marketing, research, and reading.

List each task that you must regularly perform in order to do business. Follow this by ranking each task as important, neutral or unimportant.

For instance, do you attend networking meetings? Analyze what type of business, if any, that you have gained from these meetings over the past year. Take that number and divide it into the time you spent attending, including drive time and prep time. If the monetary rewards are greater than the amount of time spent, label this task as important. If not, you get the picture. . .

---

addSpace Beginning Action Steps

Take a deep breath and analyze everything in your schedule.
Ask yourself these questions:

1. Do I need to do this task to become successful or fulfilled?
2. Why did I initially add this task to my life and is that reason still valid?
3. When was the last time I did it?

If the hours spent on a task outweigh the results, remove it from your schedule. Many people attend meetings but don't analyze the results to see if the time investment pays off financially.

If you have to attend mandatory meetings, make sure to show up with *your* agenda planned in advance. Know what you want to accomplish during this meeting: getting specific questions answered, enlisting help from co-workers or making personal or business connections.

Always have your goal in mind before you enter the meeting room, and this potential time drain will become beneficial to you.

One of my very enterprising clients, Trish, loves to network, but a few years ago she felt that she wasn't getting as much as she could from her time spent networking. She wanted to make the most of networking events and began to do what she calls "netweaving," or building bridges between the people when she met. She became a trusted resource for others who wanted to build business relationships. Trish now spends her energy on her newest creation, an Internet networking calendar of events. Her business is booming, and she is in the process of creating several more in other parts of the country.[26] She focuses her energy and time on what others need most (to connect with others) and has

> If the hours spent
> on a task outweigh
> the results, remove
> it from your
> schedule.

multiplied her networking time by becoming a resource for others.

We all want to spend our time making money, not necessarily being busy, right? Analyze the results of the time you spend in each meeting and decide if you should keep that meeting on your agenda.

This same strategy should be applied to advertising. I digress for a moment into advertising because many of my clients have failed to factor in the time they spend creating and proofing ads, as well as the analysis to determine whether an ad was actually worth their investment.

When I help set up a QuickBooks chart of accounts for clients, I often discover that their money steadily flows out but doesn't flow in at the same pace. One area where I consistently see money draining out into a black hole is advertising. As an advertising sales veteran, I caution you to only run ads if you are willing to devote the time and energy to track their success rate.

Never run an advertisement without determining a means to analyze your results. Make sure to tag each advertisement with a code so you know which ad delivered new business.

How to Say No to New Opportunities

Always pause before adding a new obligation to your agenda. The easiest method for doing this is to say that you have to check your schedule and you will get back to the person the next day. Do not let yourself be taken in by spur-of-the-moment opportunities or pressures. If it is a good opportunity, it will still be available for you another time.

Women in particular have a hard time saying no. We are typically born to nurture and often feel that saying no is showing our weakness or inability to be superwomen. Sometimes we want to show that we care by supporting others' endeavors.

What we don't realize is that not learning how to say no is a sign of weakness. Even though a survey by Vital Stats determined that 60% of Americans feel they do not have enough time to get everything done, 40% still fail to realize that they cannot accomplish everything on their schedule. Not knowing how to say no causes continual frustration and the feeling of inadequacy.

Realize that if you agree to add another recurring task to your schedule, you probably need to let go of something else.

New Opportunity #1
The Fire Drill

Every so often, we are confronted with an incredibly pressing issue that is a result of someone else's failure to perform. Their project now slides into our life and tries to become our problem. When urgent projects arise out of the blue and swiftly manifest into your life, it pays to step back a moment before reacting. Typically, it has become a personal fire alarm for the person who let it slip through the cracks. They turn to you to help them save the day. With a little time out and refreshed perspective, you will see that their predicament really has nothing to do with you.

We all want to help fellow human beings, and you might decide to do just that. Take the time to look at the task objectively and determine whether you want to help the person by letting them help themselves. Ultimately, you might decide to set aside one of your projects or goals to help them reach theirs.

The main point is this: your choice is best made, not under fire, but with objectivity and consideration. Don't get sucked into someone else's drama until you have taken the time to stop and make a conscious decision to help.

Don't get sucked into someone else's drama until you have taken the time to stop and make a conscious decision to help.

Success in Recording Your Appointments

Once you determine which activities you need to schedule, you also need to decide what type of scheduling tool you will use to keep your appointments and commitments organized.

One of the most important tools for an organized businessperson is a proper scheduling device. Whatever you choose, use ONE and ONLY ONE for everything in your life: all of your business appointments, reminder notes and personal commitments.

Your schedule can be as simple as an agenda book or a day planner, or as complicated as a Palm Pilot, Blackberry or iPhone.

As a road warrior/travel writer, I relied on my palm-sized Day Timer booklet to record my tasks and appointments. Although my techie husband has given me several electronic palm devices over the years, I still insist on using the old-fashioned pen and paper technique to record my appointments and "to do" lists. There is something about making a list and crossing off items that give me a far greater degree of satisfaction than the time I might save by inputting my client information into a computer device. As a visual/tactile learner, I always remember things more easily when I write them and read them later in my own handwriting.

Many creative people find it easier to remember

the location where they wrote a note on the page (for example, on the bottom of the left-hand page) instead of remembering the date they wrote it into their agenda. A client of mine can point to the part of the page that she wrote the note into her schedule book but could never remember the date on which she wrote it. Analytical types are more likely to remember a note on the date on which they wrote the note. This is why they are more likely to be successful using a handheld electronic device.

> In short, we are all predisposed to remember things in a certain way. You do not have to go digital unless it suits your thought process. Simply make sure that whatever scheduling device you choose, you use one and only one!

If you choose paper, make sure that it is in a format that you can always have close at hand. The agenda that I currently use is a 5x7 format so that it fits into my briefcase or purse when I am not working. If I receive a phone call, my agenda is always on hand to schedule an appointment or jot down a quick note.

With paper, you must also be diligent to list phone numbers beside your scheduled appointments because you don't have the convenience of carrying your database within a handheld electronic device. For tactile/visual learners, the reward of writing and scratching off completed tasks is worth the extra notes and data entry time.

If you choose a handheld electronic device, choose one that will "hot sync" or import/export with the information in your computer contact management program.

Whichever method you choose, paper or electronic, make sure to spend the time it requires to keep your information updated. Managing your contact list and business card collection will put you two steps closer to truly being in control of your business.

Action Steps to Master Your Schedule

1. Make a list of every task that you perform on a regular basis.
2. Group these tasks into similar categories:
    a. Calls to make.
    b. Meetings to attend.
    c. Planning and forecasting, etc.
3. Umbrella each day of the week for specific sets of related tasks.
4. Eliminate or delegate the tasks that do not move you towards your goal. Analyze each task and see if the reward is greater than the time spent.
5. Learn to say no.
6. Choose your one and only one scheduling device—never use more than one calendar!

Ole'

Now that you have analyzed your business tasks and optimized your schedule, you will need to learn how to create goals and develop the ability to stay focused and nurture them until they reach fruition.

• Notes •

Chapter Seven

....

**Mastering Your
Goals Through
Thought, Speech
and Action**

"You got to be
careful if you don't
know where you're
going, because you
might not get there."
—YOGI BERRA

Read This Chapter First If You Resonate With These Questions:

Does your business fall short of your expectations?

. . . .

Are you still light years away from manifesting your grandest dreams?

. . . .

Have you lost sight of the initial vision or picture for your success?

In the words of mastermind author Napoleon Hill, "First comes thought, then organization of that thought into ideas and plans, then transformation of those plans into reality. The beginning, as you will observe, is in your imagination."[27]

We often think that we have to *Just Do It!* to make our life and business goals happen. We jump into action, load up our schedule, get really busy and hope that we are making progress towards our goal as we go

Be careful to avoid the *busyness* syndrome, and don't work for work's sake without clear results pictured and laid out in your mind.

about our busyness. Did you notice that I did not use the word *business*? Sometimes we are too caught up in frantic activity to see if we are even on the right track. We can often easily relate to the Eveready bunny that just bangs on and on and never really reaches the goal. Be careful to avoid the *busyness* syndrome, and don't work for work's sake without clear results pictured and laid out in your mind.

Unfortunately, *busyness* is a common scenario for those who do not specify and map out their goals in advance. They inevitably spend more time and effort *just doing it* than is necessary to reach their goals. Yogi Berra said it succinctly, "You got to be careful if you don't know where you're going, because you might not get there."

In this chapter, I will share strategies to help you develop the ability to visualize your highest priority goals, write and talk about them confidently and move towards them with focused action steps until your dreams are realized.

You Already Have a Blueprint for Success

You have already accomplished one major goal in your lifetime. How do I know this? Unless you were born with a disability, you learned to walk! Have you ever considered what it takes to learn how to walk? Scientists who have studied the human act of walking consider it an extreme improbability that humans ever learn how to do it. The definition of walking is "controlled falling forward."[28] Walking is both passive and dynamic. In order to walk, humans fall and then catch themselves as they move forward. They have their eye on the place where they want to go and move towards it. Guess what? This is essentially the same process that is involved with achieving goals. Even if you have never been able to physically walk, I would wager that you have probably accomplished other large goals because of, and in spite of, your physical challenges.

Looking Back to Fall Forward

Begin by remembering three goals you have successfully reached in the past. Think about what they were and how you reached them. Did you have a formalized game plan? Did you see the end result clearly in your mind before you started? I would wager that at least one, if not both, of these statements was true for you. This is why you are able to attain your goals.

---

addSpace Action Steps

List three of your accomplishments on the margins of this page. Write down the steps you took and the end result.

See It Clearly

When we take the time to strategize and map out the game plan necessary to accomplish the end result, we are much more likely to succeed. Add the almost magical ingredient of "seeing it as so" before it becomes reality, and you will become very powerful. When you combine both techniques, the result is almost guaranteed.

When I finally met my true love and decided to marry, we were older than your average couple. My mother had died when I was young, and my father was unaware about his duties as the father of the bride. Like most women, I had a clear picture in my mind of what our wedding would look like. Unfortunately, our budget, or lack thereof, did not come close to matching my vision.

I plotted, planned and schemed about how to pull off the wedding of my dreams. I wrote it all down, expense by expense. I created the experience visually in my mind, from the fabulous dress to the beautiful ceremony and huge party surrounded by friends.

To make a long story short, I had goals, major financial goals to create the event of a lifetime! Somehow, without the help of charitable donations or an unexpected windfall, we were able to pull off a $45,000 wedding on a mere $13,000 budget accumulating no credit card debt.

We had a theatrical setting on the water, fireworks, fabulous food, harpist, guitarist, DJ, videographer, photographer, cascading flowers and, of course, the fabulous gown!

How did this happen? I know it helped immensely that the event was so well-visualized and seasoned in my brain that it simply had to come to fruition. I knew how it would look, who would attend, and that my father, the minister, would be the one to walk me down the aisle before he turned around and performed the marriage ceremony. That was one part of the wedding that was complimentary, of course! I plotted and planned and kept a running ledger as we saved during the months prior to the wedding.

Friends flew in from all over the U.S. Many helped me complete final projects during the week before and filled the void of the unbudgeted wedding planner. I still remember with huge gratitude how my girlfriends flew in and took turns keeping me focused on the list of tasks and pitching in wholeheartedly to complete the final details. Each took one or two-day shifts before they passed off the task list to the next person and then shuffled off for a mini-vacation before returning for the wedding. It definitely didn't hurt that we were living in Florida at the time!

Just like planning a major event, the key to success

is giving your unconscious mind a visible path to your goal. Being unclear about how you will reach your goal will bring about unclear results.

So, think about everything that you need to do to get what you want. Visualize it happening right before your eyes, on the movie screen of your mind. Henry David Thoreau instructed us well when he wrote, "Thought is the sculptor who can create the person you want to be."

Think and Speak Specifics

Create a mission statement for your goal. Effective mission statements should include components such as values, vision and purpose. One of my clients, Steve, created this mission, "My mission is to help others to grow personally, professionally, emotionally and spiritually by using my compassion, my unique perspective and my belief in others' inherent goodness and enormous potential." Create your own. Learn to say it aloud to yourself and others. Be specific and keep it simple. How many vacations or how much revenue do you wish to make in what period of time? Think about your goals in the way that comes naturally to you. Some think short term, some think long.

Although I'm not an avatar, sometimes I see a goal and it magically manifests without all of the baby steps in between. It can be done! I would wager that, if you were to seriously consider the accomplishments in your life, you have also done this a few times yourself. The key is to keep it so simple, clear and real in your mind that you never forget what it is that you are aiming for. You also need to state it clearly and frequently to yourself and others and see it "as so" on a daily basis. Enough metaphysical science for now . . .

Write the Path to Your Goal

Lay out your vision step-by-step in your mind and write all that you see on a piece of paper. When you write down the path to your goal, keep it simple but add as many details as you see.

If you are one of those people who don't bother writing their goals because they always fail, realize this: those people who do write their goals on paper will actually accomplish some, if not all of them. I have a friend Kevin, from South Africa who always has a list of 10 goals in writing at any given time. This is what he wrote to me about his life:

"When I was young, I figured out my life somehow played out in cycles of seven years. I decided then to create a plan to include 10 definitive objectives that would manifest into tangible goals that I could achieve within each seven-year period. If I didn't reach some goals, it was okay because they rolled over into the next period. So, in essence, I had this ferris wheel of hope and desire that always seemed full of ideas. The tools to accomplish this was the key . . . I had immediate and weekly goals that served my monthly goals, which in turn made my seven-year plan reachable. 'Start small but visualize big' is my motto I suppose."

A few of the goals Kevin has accomplished to date includes getting his green card without an attorney and, against all odds, after the terrorist attacks of 9/11, taking a camping holiday through Europe, hiking the Grand Canyon (which he has now done three times) and meeting his childhood hero, Mohammed Ali, in person, by simply knocking on his door.

It helps to surround yourself with visionaries. Their ability to reach their own lofty goals affirms that you can do the same.

Everyone visualizes the progress towards an end result differently. The analytical businessperson might plot their progress in percentages towards the goal. Artistic creative types might find the most rewarding tracking method is a graph that allows them to see their progression to the final outcome.

There is no perfect single method for accomplishing your goals. Your chosen path simply needs to motivate you and allow you to see and feel clearly defined results every step along the way. This visible progress will keep you motivated and enthusiastic as you move towards your goal.

Keeping goals simple and definable means that they are organizable. As Epictetus said: "First say to yourself what you would be; and then do what you have to do." I would add a side note to this statement. Being organized and having the path clearly defined as you proceed towards your goal is invaluable. This way, if something does go awry, you can shift and still move toward your goal, even if from a different direction, because it has become crystal clear in your thoughts. You might need to tack away from the wind, but your course will still remain true.

> Being organized and having the path clearly defined as you proceed towards your goal is invaluable.

Divide and Conquer

Simplify your path by chunking your goals into small time increments. For instance, if you want to gross $300,000 this year, divide that into 12 months, and then into the number of days you will work towards that goal each month.

Clearly dividing your end result into smaller increments will keep you from becoming overwhelmed. It will also enable you to easily track your progress on a daily basis.

This is the thinking part of thought, word and deed. You will need to think about the specific desired result at the end of each day, week, month, quarter and year.

Once you have chunked your goal into bite-sized pieces, you can go about your business and reach your incremental goals at a consistent pace. If there comes a day that your goals are not met, you can then easily make a choice to work late or add more time to your schedule the following day. You might even decide that your progress is sufficient and personal balance is more important. This is the beauty of having clearly defined steps: you can make an informed decision and sometimes choose balance without guilt because you know exactly where you are with your goals at that moment.

addSpace TIPS

Clearly divide your end result into small time increments. Start with your big picture goal and then chunk it into: quarterly, monthly, weekly and daily goals.

Take Action
Make it Real!

Define the results you want at the end of each week and write down the steps necessary to achieve them. After that, organize the steps by priority or highest impact.

For instance, to gain two new clients every week, you might need to contact 10 new prospects. To book four appointments each week, you may need to block four hours a week for the actual meetings and another two hours for follow-up calls. To develop a consistent referral-generating source, you might need to ask clients regularly for referrals, set up an email newsletter to keep in touch regularly or send notes.

Keep the Faith

Just like a baby, take small steps and keep moving even if you fall or fail a few times. As Vince Lombardi said, "If you can't accept losing, you can't win."

When I sailed in the Gulf of Mexico, the popular saying was *If you haven't run aground, you haven't really sailed the Gulf.* The water is so shallow for miles and miles offshore that you will most likely get stuck in the sand at some point. Running aground could be seen as a setback, but this has rarely stopped sailors from sailing those beautiful waters! Setbacks are a fact of life.

Think about what you really want, write it down and state it clearly to others and take daily actions to reach your goal. This practice will move you towards your dreams at jet speed, and you will soon find that you have achieved your goals with less effort than you anticipated!

Think about what you really want, write it down and state it clearly to others and take daily actions to reach your goal.

For serial entrepreneurs, the passion for reaching a goal is usually stronger after each failure. This is what helps small businesses succeed when it appears impossible to others. They learn from each setback and try again. Keep your vision of success, remain on the trail of your true intention and you will surely succeed. Godspeed!

---

addSpace Action Steps

Think it—Write It—Speak it—to Achieve it!

1. Think about your current long-term and short-term goals.
2. See them clearly in your mind.
3. Write them down.

There are other ways to achieve your goals. If you are a "big picture" person, you can visualize your goal, keeping your eye on it while allowing no distractions; work every day with that goal in mind, and it materializes. As you become more experienced at manifesting your goals, you will reach a plateau where, occasionally, you can go straight to the end result by seeing your goal as already accomplished, talking about it as if it's so, and acting as if it is your reality. And so it will be . . . before you know it!

Chapter Eight

Create a
Masterful
Image

"To begin creating a new wardrobe, you need to first add space by clearing out the old clothes that no longer fit your body shape or your career or personal goals."

Read This Chapter First If You Resonate With These Questions:

Is your closet bulging with old clothes and no space to add new clothes that fit and flatter your current body?

· · · · · · · · · · · · · · · · ·

Does your wardrobe no longer fit who you aspire to be?

· · · · · · · · · · · · · · · · ·

Are you confused about how to choose clothes that make you feel unstoppable in the world?

Your image is created by your thoughts and feelings about yourself. If you have never taken the time to pause and figure out how you feel about yourself and how you want to be viewed by the world, it will be reflected in your wardrobe. The clothes you wear can sabotage or support what you want to create in your life.

Clothes not only reflect how we feel about ourselves, they also impact how others react to us. Whether you are a man or a woman, you are judged by the clothes that you wear. This is a reality. The power of a first impression is real and does not diminish for some time. This might seem cruel and unreasonable until you realize why this happens.

We don't make quick character judgments because we are malicious. We do it because it is one of our most primal instincts, self-protection. We are programmed to determine as quickly as possible whether the person next to us is trustworthy, or if we should take a flight-or-fight stance. We simply rely on visual clues to determine whether we are safe.

During this instinctive process, we can't help but make other judgments about professionalism, financial status and personality. Knowing this, it makes sense that we should try to appear as polished as possible. It is not a secret that a successful and positive personal image is a direct result of the clothes we wear.

Creating a successful image goes a lot deeper than outward appearances. Clothes change the way we view ourselves. Think about your wardrobe for a minute. Almost everyone has a lucky piece of clothing. When we wear that item our attitude throughout the day is more self-assured. That is why we really enjoy wearing our "lucky" outfits. We feel happier and more successful. With the proper elements in your wardrobe, you will

Creating a successful image goes a lot deeper than outward appearances. Clothes change the way we view ourselves.

feel empowered every day as you get dressed and head out into the world.

> *This chapter will provide a step-by-step guide to:*
> 1. Get clear on who you are/aspire to be.
> 2. Review and revise your image goals.
> 3. Create space in your wardrobe to enable change.
> 4. Choose the wardrobe that brings out the best in you.

Get Clear on Where You're Heading

Just as many ideas that we hold about ourselves also no longer represent who we really are, many clothes that we wear don't fit our life anymore, physically or mentally. Everyone has inherited or limiting ideas lurking in our subconscious that are simply no longer truths. Take a minute to think about what inherited values might be holding you back. It is probable that if you now take a look at your present wardrobe, you will find a reflection of those old ideas there as well.

For instance, if you grew up hearing and then believing that money does not grow on trees or is hard to come by, you probably still have outdated clothes in your closet that are 10 to 20 years old. You might find

it incredibly hard to release these old items because tossing them out would be "wasting" hard-earned money. These beliefs and "self-talk" can hinder the process of creating a new image for yourself.

A polished image is more than just looking good—it helps you take on challenges with greater confidence. Something magical happens when you put on the perfect clothes for your body type, coloring and lifestyle. A dot. com client, Mike, was in the process of launching his new venture and also searching for companionship and love. After spending several months in the isolation of product creation, it was time for him to step out into the world and unveil his product and himself as a successful entrepreneur. Mike wanted to create an image that reflected how he now perceived himself and his new venture. He was, in essence, redefining himself as a confident professional and self-sufficient entrepreneur.

After clearing out his old wardrobe and making room for the new, he began learning what he could wear to portray his new image and lifestyle. After learning to apply the principles contained in this chapter, he wrote, "I realized I had . . . been wasting gobs of money on clothes that weren't making me look better. Not only do I now have a wardrobe full of clothes that are flattering, I also have the knowledge to make more savvy purchases . . . [and] my new girlfriend (who was a runway model for Ralph Lauren) has complimented me on my fashion sense more than once."

For Mike, wearing the right clothes went deeper than just looking good and saving money. His wardrobe has bolstered his confidence and given him courage to pursue his dreams with no holds barred. Who wouldn't want to proclaim that his girlfriend was a model for Ralph Lauren? With the right wardrobe and understanding a few basic principles about how to dress to enhance his image, he now has the confidence to present himself and his new business boldly to the world.

What is the life that you wish to create? Do you want to be physically fit or more successful? Maybe your goal is to find a life partner or become more adventuresome? Get clear on the current top priorities for your life. These will guide you in your choices about your personal style.

How Do You Want to Show Up?

There is an easy way to redefine and create the style that you wish to present to the world. Fashion is often divided into four types of styles: classic, sporty, trendy or romantic. Most of us feel comfortable in a combination of one or two of these styles. A few of us will change styles completely according to our mood on any given day.

> Get clear on the current top priorities for your life. These will guide you in your choices about your personal style.

Classic stylization is based on clean, structured lines with minimal embellishment. Sporty styles include clothing made in fabrics that are flexible and breathable. Romantic styles often include soft lines, lace and frills. Trendy is the toughest category to master and requires constant diligence to the world's perception of what is "in" and what is "out" of style.

As a classic stylist, I believe the easiest way to show your personal style and power is to include the essential clothing elements in your wardrobe. The basic clothing elements for men and women are written in a special report available in the order form in the back of this book and also at www.addspacetoyourlife.com/my-book.

With these items in your closet, you can accessorize to match your personal style, mood and goals, whether in the guise of the classic, romantic, sporty or trendsetter.

Once the basic wardrobe elements are a part of your life, you can experiment to your heart's content and still project a polished image to the world.

Wearing a different blouse or shirt with the same suit can completely change the image you project. If you own a suit that fits your body perfectly and is constructed in the right color with simple lines in a good fabric, you can transform your image with minimal effort. For instance, how would you view a man in a suit with a white shirt and red tie versus a man in the same suit wearing a silk t-shirt? Which shirt would best represent a successful businessman during a sales presentation? Which shirt would be more appropriate for a cocktail party? How much power do you think the salesman would embrace if he wore that silk t-shirt during his boardroom presentation?

As a romantic, you can express your personality with a ruffled blouse under a classic suit. If modern and trendy is your current state of mind, accessorize the suit with the most fashionable shoes, earrings or belt to let the world know that you are hip, current and forward thinking. As an artist who wants to be taken seriously, show your artistic flair with a carefully placed accessory on a classic item. Combine a large sparkly brooch with a classic sheath dress. A good rule of thumb is to wear only one exceptional item of clothing per outfit.

Clothing affects our choices and moods throughout the day. If you aspire to work out more and lose weight, perhaps embodying a sporty style in your off-work hours will help you get in gear to exercise more. This is why savvy "work at home" professionals who never see clients in person each morning get showered and dressed before they sit down at their home computer to begin the day's work.

Regularly review your goals and examine whether

> Clothing affects our choices and moods throughout the day.

your wardrobe still reflects who you are and who you aspire to become. Setting the stage with your wardrobe will help accelerate your movement towards your goals. Your image and wardrobe are intricately related to the big picture of who you really are.

Create Space in Your Closet

To begin creating a new wardrobe, you need to first add space by clearing out the old clothes that no longer fit your body shape or your career or personal goals. According to a study by IKEA, "Cleaning out your closet has often been rated more satisfying than sex."[29] This is because adding space and releasing old clothes also releases old patterns and perceptions. I watch clients frequently become excited, energized and joyful as they release old clothes and clutter.

It is obvious that where there is clutter, there is stagnant energy. Things cannot move, often literally. Perhaps there is not enough physical space to push aside the suit in your closet to access a specific shirt. This area is jammed and stuck which makes you frustrated. You will most likely even lose the desire to wear that shirt. The energy surrounding that shirt is now effectively closed down.

This "stuckness" is probably part of the reason that we only wear 20% of the clothes that we own. It takes less energy to access the frequently worn clothes in the front of the closet than the ones in the back. Sometimes we will even default to wearing the clothes that haven't yet made their way back into the closet from the laundry. These clothes have huge amounts of fresh energy surrounding them! Sound familiar?

Get Your Tools in Place

It helps to enlist the help of a professional or a friend whose fashion judgment you respect. Realize that if you choose a family member for this process, you will be in danger of dealing with old energy patterns surrounding your relationship with this person and with the items at hand.

If your mother helps you, her viewpoint might be skewed and sentimental about certain items. If your sister helps, she might harbor feelings of jealousy and unconsciously not want you to look your best. The best person to help you with this part of the process is a professional.

Hiring an Image Consultant will save you thousands of dollars because you will no longer buy items that you will never wear. You will be armed with the knowledge of what you should buy to look your best. If hiring a professional is currently beyond your means, choose a friend, man or woman, whose fashion judgment you

Hiring an Image Consultant will save you thousands of dollars because you will no longer buy items that you will never wear.

respect and who will also be brutally honest about how each piece of clothing fits and looks on your body.

> Other tools to have on hand:
> - Boxes for donations.
> - Bags for repairs, alterations and laundry.
> - Pad of paper and pen.

Begin by Eliminating

The only real way to know if a piece of clothing works for you now is to try it on and listen to someone else's advice. You cannot truly see your backside, even with a 360-degree mirror, and it's almost impossible to be objective about your own clothes. There is always a history with each item that will cloud your judgment when deciding to keep or release.

Begin to try on each piece of clothing to see if it fits and is in good shape. If it does fit and also reflects the image you wish to project, place it back in your closet. If it does not fit your current body or lifestyle, place it in the donation box. If a small alteration or repair will make it work for you, place it in the alterations box. Keep this in mind: if an item has seen its glory days but you still want to keep it: *You are too good to wear clothing that is worn out or has holes.* If it needs cleaning, is still

You are too good to wear clothing that is worn out or has holes.

in good shape and skims your body in all of the right places, place it in the dry cleaning bag or hamper.

Items that are totally unsalvageable (i.e., old stretched out and faded sweaters, shirts with perspiration stains, etc.) get tossed in the trash. Garments that are poor quality, itch or are in oversupply (t-shirts often make up this category) should go into the tax-deductible charity box.

Make sure to investigate and unload your dresser and all clothing drawers in this process. Take the time to eliminate socks without mates, hose with runs and old, stretched bras and undies.

addSpace TIPS

For Women

If you have never been professionally fitted for a bra or haven't done so in the past year, schedule an appointment with your local bra expert. (Nordstrom bra fitters are very well trained.) Approximately 80% of women are currently wearing the wrong size bra. A good bra will position your breasts to sit slightly higher than half way between your shoulders and elbow. Clothes fit amazingly better when the "betties" are hoisted!

Take Notes

As you sort, make a list of which items you need to replace and which ones need coordinating pieces. I have developed the *Essential Wardrobe Elements Report* which can be purchased in the back order form.

For Men

Make sure to spend your money wisely on your shoes. Men are frequently judged by the shoes they wear. Invest the extra money on good leather Italian construction. It shows! Take the time every week to clean your shoes and belt.

Choose Clothes That Will Enhance Your Image

Once your closet is clear of the old, unwanted items, it is time to choose the most flattering items for who you are right now. Your complexion, eyes and hair color will help you determine your basic color palette. As a classic stylist, I choose one of three neutral color palettes for each client—navy, brown or black—and begin coordinating a solid wardrobe from there. To determine your base color, ask your friend/stylist or go to the best department store in your area and ask a sales associate. Once you choose your base color, concentrate your energies by investing in classic wardrobe items in this color. Purchase accessories in other colors that complement your base color choice.

addSpace TIPS

To determine your base color, hold each of the three neutral colors up to your face and notice whether your face recedes or comes forward with each color choice. This might be difficult to see for yourself. If you can't tell which color is best, ask a friend to help. Check it in natural light, preferably outside so you can see the true results.

There are two books that I recommend to clients who want more detailed advice about their colors. The first is the long-running industry standard, *Color Me Beautiful,* by Carol Jackson. There is also a more recent book published by two colleagues that presents a thoughtful and intriguing new definition of color and style. Jesse Garza and Joe Lupo have created *Life in Color: The Visual Therapy Guide to the Perfect Palette—For Your Clothes, Your Makeup, and You!*.[30] This book is a great read if you want to learn more about your color and personal style.

Skim and Never Cling

Proper fit is the most important aspect of great style. Clothes that skim your bodylines are the most flattering.

For the majority of people, "off the rack" clothes do not fit perfectly. In fact, clothes on store racks are only designed to fit 2% of our population. After all, how many perfect size 6 women do you know? Also, how many men do you know that fall neatly into the 5'9"/170 pound bracket? Most people don't think about having their clothes altered. Once you appreciate how the retail clothing industry operates, however, you will also realize that, more likely than not, you will need to get some aspect of the clothes you buy off the rack tailored to fit your unique body shape.

For the most part, everyone has one particular body part that does not fall into the norm. Perhaps your arms are short or your chest is very large or one leg is longer than the other. This is NORMAL! It is not normal to fit perfectly into mass-manufactured clothing. Once you develop a relationship with a good tailor, you are a short step away from creating a more polished image.

Clothes should skim and never cling to your body—especially the areas you are self-conscious about. Most of us have at least one area that we wish we could minimize or make disappear. This is the area that you want to de-emphasize. This does not mean covering it up with oversized clothes, it means complementary lines and fabric seaming.

I find that many of my male clients dress at least

one size too large saying they want to be comfortable. In fact, the word *comfortable* is the vex of most image consultants. Many people choose the wrong clothes simply because comfort is their main priority. Who is considered powerful and professional when the image they portray is comfortable? The folks living day to day in "comfortable" clothes are the ones still waiting to make a mark on the world.

What most people don't realize is that being comfortable is not about wearing a larger size, but simply wearing clothes that fit in all of the right places and are proportionate to your body shape. If your clothes skim, don't cling and are made of good fabric, they are typically comfortable enough to sleep in.

After losing 50 pounds, my client Liz, a professional clown (yes, she was paid to clown around for a living), came to me to help her revamp her wardrobe. She had spent years in her glitzy alter ego and was ready to step into a new phase of her life as a caregiver and women's empowerment facilitator. While perusing her closet, I discovered a collection of flowing oversized clothes. This woman was literally hiding her new and improved body in loose clothes that flowed to the floor. She thought she was hiding her self-perceived flaws behind her wardrobe when, in reality, she was making herself appear larger than life.

Many people choose the wrong clothes simply because comfort is their main priority.

As Liz was trying on the new clothes I selected for her, she was amazed to discover that she was a petite. Even though she is 5'2", she had never visited a petite department or tried on clothes that were the proper length in the arms, torso or legs. She now avoids baggy, ill-fitting clothes and her new wardrobe has taken another 30 pounds off of her appearance.

Do you think Liz now feels more powerful, inspired and energetic? You bet! Here is what Liz said: "It's been an epiphany working with you. We get so comfortable with what we know. We go a size larger thinking it will make us look smaller when, in fact, it does the opposite. I really see that now. Investing in clothes for myself is now a simple and easy task. I have the knowledge to know what works for me and what to avoid. I have been receiving many compliments on my newly acquired fashion and style."

Although you may feel that your clothes express your personality, and they might, it pays to step back and evaluate your level of professionalism as expressed through your wardrobe. Many artists have created a personal image that becomes an obstacle to their success. There is a disconnection between their incredible talents and the way they present themselves visually to the world.

Don't let your appearance block your success. Find

a friend whose fashion judgment you trust, or hire a professional to help you upgrade your current wardrobe. Try on every piece of clothing in your closet. Check to see that they still fit not only your body, but also the image you wish to create.

When Should You Review Your Image?

You should always remain diligent about the image you project by the clothes you wear. Just like any other major aspect of your life, review it regularly to see if it is in alignment with your goals. Any time that you have a career or life transition, consider how your clothes affect your transformation. Will they enable your new life or detract from it?

One of my clients, Gina, is a biotech scientist who wanted to advance her career. She realized that even though her colleagues and the next-level managers often wore jeans and tennis shoes, she was not gaining the respect of the upper-level managers dressed that way. When we switched her day-to-day attire to coordinates taken from suits combined with dressier shirts, she received new management responsibilities within six months. Gina told me: "I am not sure if the new image had anything to do with my promotion, but I am certain that it has helped me to be taken more seriously at work. My eyes were opened to realize that I was not dressing as well as the other management-level associates in my company. Looking back, I don't know why I did not see that on my own, but I didn't! I guess it is very difficult to see yourself objectively."

One year and two promotions later in her new wardrobe, Gina has progressed from managing a staff of seven to heading a department of 42!

Get the help you need, be it from a trusted friend or professional image consultant and know that you can express your unique talents and personality and still maintain an air of authority. It never hurts to appear more polished and professional. Your clothes do make your first impression. Spend the time to create a purposeful image that shows off how unique and magnificent you truly are!

> *Remember this point, sent to me from colleagues Joe and Jesse at Visual-Therapy:*
> "What you put out there is a direct reflection of how you feel inside. Taking time to care for your appearance and your image is a form of self-respect; do not be afraid to ask for help or hire professionals to bring you to the next level."
> —Joe Lupo and Jesse Garza, Co-Founders of Visual-Therapy and authors of *Life in Color: The Visual Guide to the Perfect Palette—for Fashion, Beauty, and You!*

addSpace Wardrobe Action Steps

1. Get clear on who you want to become and what changes you want in your life.

2. Get a professional or friend whose fashion-sense you trust to help you purge your wardrobe and shop.

3. Create space in your closet.

4. Go through your current wardrobe piece by piece. Take a good look at each item to see if it fits you and the life you want to create.

5. Shop for items that skim and don't cling to your body.

6. Purchase your main essential clothing elements in one of the three base neutral colors: brown, navy or black.

7. Be aware of the image you project and how it supports your success.

8. Review your wardrobe and image at least once a year and whenever you make a major life transition.

• Notes •

Chapter Nine

Masters Hire
Other Masters

"Enlist the support
of others to help
you move forward
in whatever areas
of your life are not
flourishing."

Read This Chapter First If You Resonate With These Questions:

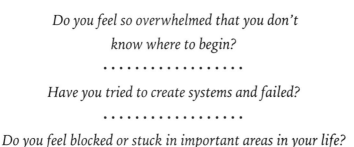

Do you feel so overwhelmed that you don't know where to begin?

. . . .

Have you tried to create systems and failed?

. . . .

Do you feel blocked or stuck in important areas in your life?

Sometimes you may feel so overwhelmed that you don't know where to start. If your physical and mental space is cluttered, it is extremely difficult to think about the important matters at hand. You can't figure out where to begin because you are distracted by the clutter, unfinished tasks and thoughts preoccupying your mind.

Instead of overwhelming stress, your response to chaos and disorganization might be irritation. This irritation might take up space in your mind that you

would otherwise use to create a new theory or product to sell to the world.

Frequently, there is also shame attached to your muck, some sense of unworthiness or undeservedness. You might constantly berate yourself with harsh thoughts about your inability to create systems to contain your possessions. You might feel that you don't deserve to have a family or lover because you can't keep your own life in order.

If organizing your papers or clearing the closet feels harder than you think it should, this is normal. When you feel overwhelmed and unable to master a small, seemingly insignificant task, don't beat yourself up. It might look like something small on the outside, but if you haven't been able to follow through on your own, it is probably linked to something much larger on the inside.

When you come up against this resistance, have compassion for yourself. In fact, resistance or feelings of anxiety are actually a sign that you are getting close to a breakthrough and the possibility for a great transformation. For example, perhaps you have an overcrowded closet. You know that you should deal with this area because your door won't close and you can't find anything that you need. You might think your challenge is simply the jam-packed closet. In reality, the deeper issue is that you frequently shop when you feel lonely. Once your closet is cleared out, you will probably realize how much money you have wasted on the clothes you never wore. You might also start thinking about how you managed to get into this situation. At that point, you might decide to stop shopping to fill your time and bring more people into your life by volunteering or starting a new class. Shopping was your band-aid, your overcrowded closet was the result. Now you know that the real muck was emotional pain—your loneliness—and by clearing out your closet, you have freed yourself of both emotional and physical clutter, making space in your life for more fulfillment and love.

Change Is a Fact of Life

Life is about constant change. Sometimes we simply get tired of learning and changing and feel more comfortable staying where we are. This is why it is understandable that people get stuck. It happens to everyone at some point in his or her life. You do not have to excel in every area of your life. In fact, it is not possible. It is not in our DNA to be great at everything. Thank goodness or this would truly be a boring and one-dimensional world. It's not a tragedy if you can't figure out how to keep the paper piles at bay or get on top of whatever else is mucking up your life. You are probably great in other

Everyone
needs help
moving through
personal blocks
at one time or
another. The
most successful
people in life
realize this and
quickly hire
others to assist.

areas of your life. There is no shame in not having the "organizing" or "wardrobe gene." It is a shame, however, if you don't enlist the help of others to overcome your lack of innate talents in whatever areas are holding you back from success. Enlist the support of others to help you move forward in whatever areas of your life are not flourishing.

Everyone needs help moving through personal blocks at one time or another. The most successful people in life realize this and quickly hire others to assist them when they reach a personal or career standstill.

Pros can help you shift much more easily and effortlessly than you could on your own. Inviting a new energy into your life with someone that is not attached to your situation can have a profound effect. A Professional Organizer or Image Consultant is not caught up in the stories you are telling yourself about why you can't let go of muck or make changes in your life. They might make it look simple because they are not immersed in your life. They have no attachments to your stuff and can see clearly where you need to begin and what you need to change to move forward. Pros are trained to help you with an outward transformation in your environment, schedule or wardrobe, which creates the space for an inner transformation. It is this inner transformation that is the true jewel of the experience.

If you feel stuck in some area of your life, be it relationships, career or health, start by clearing your environment of unnecessary objects. This is an easy place to begin. It might seem insurmountable, but the good news is that all you really need to do is start. And if you have tried and failed to take charge of your clutter, hire a professional. In a short time, a professional can help you move the papers, set up a system, create a new wardrobe or do whatever else is needed so that you can gain confidence and a new feeling of mastery. Meanwhile, you have begun to remove blocks that were holding you back from a lot more than just a clean shelf.

Create Space to Grow

If you set your intention to move forward and change, but don't let anything go, your goals will be much harder to manifest. Growth requires space. The neat thing is this: It does not matter what you clear. It can be as small as getting rid of the extra set of knives or a few appointments from an overcrowded schedule. Simply get help and begin *anywhere*. Your energy will soon shift and you will be on your way to manifesting your true potential.

Unblocking one area will lead to unblocking other much deeper areas in your life. Have you ever noticed

Growth requires space. The neat thing is this: It does not matter what you clear.

that after you clean out the junk drawer, you feel energized to tackle a much larger, totally unrelated project? Muck is much bigger than the stuff attached to it. There is a domino effect, and eventually you will arrive at the core area where you are really stifled, be it creativity, lack of productivity, depression or boredom. You will inevitably feel lighter and more creative and energized.

Peter Walsh states it succinctly in his book, *It's All Too Much*, "If you are like most people I have worked with, your stuff has, at one time or another, cluttered not only your home, but also your mind and your life . . . Once the weight has been lifted, you have the opportunity to take what you have learned in decluttering and organizing . . . and apply those principles to almost every aspect of your life: your mind, your body, your career, friendships, family and romantic relationships. You have an infinite capacity to achieve greatness. I know it, I have seen it."[31]

To demonstrate how the consequence of adding space works, I have included this brief excerpt from a note sent by a client: "Hi Kathi! Just wanted to give you a quick follow-up on my new wardrobe (and attitude)! Truthfully, I have barely recovered from the shopping experience: I've never met anyone with your energy and drive. I wonder how much your clients have expressed to you what an important part of the consultation experience it is to receive that kind of focused attention! You are unquestionably an agent of change. Not just clothing, but attitude, outlook, much deeper! Kind of like walking in expecting a dressing room, and experiencing . . . maybe a psychic wind tunnel!

I've only begun to absorb the new wardrobe, but so far the reactions I have gotten have ranged from compliments to double-takes, from my family (even my fashionista daughter), as well as my friends and co-workers. I haven't gotten promoted yet (that only comes up two times a year in my company), but I do feel bolder and think I may be stretching my wings a little.

Anyway, thank you for the advice and the whole experience . . . it is really having a ripple effect on my life! Somehow it's enabled me to tap into a vast store of energy, and since our shopping trip I have re-organized my bedroom, dining room, office at work . . . all kinds of stuff!"

I encourage you to contact a local Professional Organizer or Image Consultant to help you transform your life. A professional will help you move to the next level and create the space to master the part of your life that isn't working. Become the master of your muck and move consciously and fully into the expression of who you really are!

> A professional will help you move to the next level and create the space to master the part of your life that isn't working.

addSpace Action Steps

1. Determine what type of help you need to gain momentum with your goals.

2. Ask your friends for referrals to area professionals in your local area or visit www.napo.net, www.ProfessionalOrganizerFinder.com or www.aici.com to find accredited professionals.

3. Set up a phone interview to determine which consultant you resonate with.

4. Schedule an appointment to begin clearing your life of whatever is holding you back.

Once you become the master of your life, you might consider joining this noble industry to begin helping others master their muck. Learning to master many aspects of life is truly a life-changing experience for everyone involved! In Chapter Ten, I will offer further direction and information for those considering becoming a Professional Organizer or Image Consultant.

Chapter Ten

A Masterful
Calling

"Empowerment is
spreading throughout
our world as people
learn how to add
space and energy to
their life."

Read This Chapter First If You Resonate With These Questions:

Are you good at seeing the untapped potential in others?

. . . .

Do you enjoy creating systems to keep you and your family organized?

. . . .

Are you the person that friends frequently ask for fashion advice?

Professional Organizers help people move through far greater personal obstacles than physical clutter. Image Consultants do much more than outfit their clients in great-fitting clothes. These professions are in the process of bringing about great change to our world, one client at a time.

Both professions help people shift their thoughts about themselves and where they fit in the world. They help clients release what no longer serves them and create space for more inspired living. Space always helps people lead more successful lives. This is why I named my company *addSpace to Your Life!*

Throughout my own personal growth process, I have learned that muck has the potential to make me stuck. Any time my life is too full of time commitments, I have the tendency to become overwhelmed. It feels easier to shut down because I get exhausted simply thinking about tackling everything on my "to do" list. This is why I work on the surface level of clutter, time management and clothes. It seems superficial at first glance: simply organizing, purging, creating an optimized schedule or a new image, but I have witnessed the power behind this action in every client I have worked with.

Consider this: When a person organizes one area of their life, they feel more powerful and in control, and they begin to realize that they can manifest other things they want in their life. What's more, they have the newfound energy to do so. This attitude spreads to everyone around them. The folks they connect with also begin to believe that they can do it as well. Empowerment is spreading throughout our world as people learn how to add space and energy to their life.

Once you start a new energy pattern within a client's environment, it becomes propelled into motion

and has an eternal life. It cannot be stopped once it is ignited because this is the way of nature. It is natural to change, grow and flourish. My client, Jann, wrote this: "I asked Kathi to help with a simple organizing of my closet. It had instant impact on my life as I turned up for work the next day wearing clothes I had long forgotten I owned—great combinations not easily found in the jumble of everything hung together. With the closet clearer, I could move the things under the bed that had long bothered me to a new, more organized space in the closet. This clearing gave me great gusto—I then cleared my desk out only to find—pronto—my work life is getting more organized. I truly see how one small successful change both has a deep psychological clearing impact—a freeing of spirit—while urging more order in other areas of life. All of a sudden, I have more time for my creative endeavors. And my gusto is catching on—my boyfriend has started organizing his stuff that has been lying around, pulling on him . . . We both feel calmer and clearer and breathe a little more deeply. Kathi is doing truly profound and amazing work in the world!"

Jann's story is not unique. Most of my clients wind up teaching the skills they learn to their friends and colleagues. By passing on the skills they have learned from their consultant, they become more masterful. As it passes on to other friends, *they* also begin to feel more powerful. The ripple effect from our industry is huge. Change that begins with one person continues on as a force for growth in others. Movement and growth is a constant part of nature.

Growth Means Change

It is not natural to be stuck or stopped. This is why muck feels so uncomfortable. It can lead to a great deal of pain and impotence. It is not uncommon for clients to break down in tears or scream in rage as they begin to remove blocks. They are simply voicing their deep feelings of distress and unease with where they are at that time. There is a tremendous power that is unleashed through clearing . . . your client's muck. We are being driven crazy by the fact that our lives are clogged with possessions and stuff.

For sanity to return, we all need to clear away our personal muck so that individually, and collectively, the whole of humanity can move forward.

When you help others create space, beauty and order in their environment, you are also helping them develop a sense of worthiness for new and better things. As they experience the physical release firsthand, they become more open and receptive and able to create a better life for themselves. They will have a newfound space to help them become more masterful. Helping our clients remove blocks in one area impacts their life and the lives of those around them. The work of these professions supports the evolution of human consciousness in small but significant ways.

Spiritual teacher and author Eckhart Tolle states it this way in his book, *A New Earth: Awakening to Your Life's Purpose*: "Most people's lives are cluttered with things: material things, things to do, things to think about. Their lives are like the history of humanity, which Winston Churchill defined as 'one damn thing after another.' Their minds are filled up with a clutter of thoughts, one thought after another. This is the dimension of object consciousness that is people's predominant reality, and this is why their lives are so out of balance. Object consciousness needs to be balanced by space consciousness for sanity to return to our planet and for humanity to fulfill its destiny. The arising of space consciousness is the next stage in the evolution of humanity."[32]

Do You Love Change?

In this book, I have addressed the classic ways that people become stuck by looking at the external ways that muck manifests itself. Muck can take many different forms and appear in many different areas of our life. Most novice organizers and image consultants begin their careers as "generalists" to determine which areas they enjoy working in and also how they might best serve. I remain a generalist, with a few specialties, because, for me, it is not about the type of clutter or stuff; it is about clearing the muck it creates. My calling is to help remove whatever is holding the client back by starting on the physical level of their possessions and surroundings. Clients frequently tell me, *My possessions are possessing me!,* which is another reason to start where they feel the most pain, regardless if it is in their wardrobe, kitchen, paper piles or schedule.

If you feel that you have mastery over any of these areas, you might have found your calling by helping others master their challenges. To further explore these professions, visit the websites of the National Association of Professional Organizers (www.napo.net) and the Association of Image Consultants International (www.aici.org). You will find clubs, meetings and training programs in your area. Both of these professions focus on helping others do what they cannot do for themselves: provide clear, objective insight and direction to enable their clients to become more fulfilled and able to live their true purpose.

addSpace Action Steps

1. Explore the professional organizing or image consulting industry.
2. Visit www.napo.net or www.aici.org.
3. Interview industry professionals and their clients to learn what the career entails.
4. Attend a local chapter meeting of NAPO or AICI to learn more and meet potential colleagues.
5. Apprentice with seasoned professionals to learn the necessary skill sets.
6. Attend training programs and national professional conferences.

When the intention to help humanity embrace an inner power is held in mind, the work of Professional Organizers and Image Consultants aligns with writers like Tolle to support the evolution of humanity and human consciousness. If you hear the call, even faintly, I urge you to look further into these professions. Became a change agent and help people create the space they need in their lives to become more joyful, fulfilled human beings. The world will never stop changing. We can help teach others to co-create, embrace change and welcome it with enthusiasm and arms open wide. I invite you to share in this fulfilling and rewarding calling!

• Notes •

About the Author
Kathi Burns, CPO®
Professional Organizer,
Image Consultant & Master of Change

. . . .

Kathi Burns, CPO®, is a Board Certified Professional Organizer, Image Consultant and Syndicated Columnist. Kathi is a regular contributing guest expert for NBC 7/39 News. She also appears regularly on other TV news programs and national magazines such as *Better Homes and Gardens*. Her company, *addSpace to Your Life!* has been featured by the *Christian Broadcasting Network* as well as *Good Morning America*.

Kathi lives in North County San Diego with her husband and two cats. Her hobbies include yoga, reading, sailing and singing in a Kirtan band named Jaya!, who performs throughout Southern California and has an upcoming CD.

As the founder of *addSpace To Your Life!*, a Professional Organizing and Image Consultancy, she helps clients clear their muck and create systems to move forward in life. Kathi discovered that her dharma, or purpose in life, is helping others become masters of change. Her passion is ignited while witnessing clients gain mastery over their wardrobe or environment and begin to change their relationship with change. During the addSpace process, clients become emboldened and lose their fear of change, which makes it easier for them to overcome other personal obstacles beyond the muck of getting organized or dressing well. They create space in their lives for what truly matters to them, which in turn, gives them the vision and inspiration to live their purpose. As Kathi frequently exclaims, "What's not to love about that!"

Acknowledgements

. . . .

I gratefully acknowledge and express deep appreciation to the many incredible people who have made this book possible.

To my addSpace clients, without whom I could not have witnessed the power firsthand of adding space. Your energy, humor and dedication to creating yourself anew is awe-inspiring!

To my extraordinary editors, Jann Einfeld and Kyla Stinnett, who kept a loving and diligent vigil on my manuscript. They helped me clarify, and ironically, organize the message that I wanted to bring to the world.

To Peter Walsh, professional organizer, visionary and host of *Clean Sweep*, Clinton Kelly and Stacy London of

What Not To Wear, whose work in television has helped bring the relatively unknown professions of organizing and image consulting into the homes of America.

To my colleagues who have encouraged me with their support, friendship and professionalism.

To my publicist, Lynn Pittman. Your energy, drive and professionalism continue to inspire me.

To Joan and Matthew Greenblatt at CenterPointe Media, who kept me focused and cleared the muck of overwhelming and seemingly endless decisions as this book neared completion.

To my spiritual counselors, Rev. Alan Rowbotham, Eckhart Tolle, Rev. Tony Bonaccorso, Rev. Will Newsom, Emmet Fox, and Barbara Marx Hubbard.

Most of all, to my husband, Robert Burns, whose talent, vision and dedication behind the scenes helped create and market our company, *addSpace To Your Life!*. His love, support and friendship will always be precious and priceless.

Notes

. . . .

[1] Namasté is salutation in Sanskrit, which can be translated as, *"The light in me honors the light in you."*

[2] John F. Kennedy address in the Assembly Hall at Paulskirche in Frankfurt. June 25, 1963

[3] Siddhartha is the founder of Buddhism.

[4] Direct Marketing Association:
Visit to have your name removed from junk mail lists
http://tinyurl.com/6avn9s

[5] To order your Freedom Filer Label Kit, use the products order form in the back of this book or order online at
http://www.addspacetoyourlife.com/shop/office-organizing/

[6] Reinforced Hanging Folders:
Staples has a great line of reinforced hanging folders that competes in quality with Pendaflex. You can order them directly using this link: http://cli.gs/yUq3T0

[7] Manila File Folders:
http://tinyurl.com/cjdfpo

[8] Vertical File Holder:
http://tinyurl.com/bn9y5

[9] Bankers Boxes:
http://tinyurl.com/ano9uc

[10] NAPO, the National Association of Professional Organizers

Notes

169

has a website where you can search for an Organizer in your area. Visit http://napo.net/Referral/. You can also use this great resource: www.ProfessionalOrganizerFinder.com

[11] *Stepped vertical file folder holders are generally made from plastic-coated metal in black or sometimes chrome. Make sure the one you purchase has eight compartments and is designed as an ascending vertical staircase. You will need two if you are making both a home and business file system.* You can order using this link: http://tinyurl.com/bn9y5

[12] Marlene Hansen, *"Organizing Your Bill Paying System"*, Office Systems Magazine, http://tinyurl.com/bapw4w

[13] *Newsweek*, June 7, 2004.

[14] Sterilite Clear Plastic Storage Boxes http://tinyurl.com/b5ykhm

[15] *New York Times*, March 1, 2001.

[16] See #13 above.

[17] Vertical File Holder: http://tinyurl.com/bn9y5

[18] Of the total eight hours wasted per week in paper document management, we spend 1 hour finding documents, one hour with difficulty in sharing documents, one hour in distribution/storage and one-half hour in arching and retrieval. www.imagetag.com, 2003.

[19] Geoff Ables, *The Source*, 2003.

[20] Fifi Ball and Sally Brickell, *Business Balance Magazine*, Summer 2003.

[21] Heinz Tschabitscher, How Many Emails Are Sent Every Day? http://tinyurl.com/cs84rj

[22] The International Labor Organization, Decent Food at Work: Raising Workers' Productivity and Well-being, http://tinyurl.com/bt634n

[23] People who multitask are less efficient than those who focus on one project at a time. Time lost switching among tasks

increases with the complexity of the tasks. Star-Telegram. com, March 1, 2003.

[24] Ted Johns, *Perfect Time Management*, (Arrow Books, 1999).

[25] The average American worker is interrupted eight times an hour. Not only do they struggle to get into their creative zone, they lose productivity because they are repeating steps to retraced where they left off. Jim Miller, Extended Workplace Solutions for U.S. West Input Management Industry Statistics.

[26] Mindy Sellinger, www.NetworkingEventFinders.com

[27] Napoleon Hill (1883-1970), American author and creator of the "Philosophy of Achievement" teachings.

[28] About half of the time during a gait (walk) cycle we are not doing anything, just falling forward. Robot Unravels Mystery of Walking, Prof. Florentin Worgotter http://tinyurl.com/2958ke

[29] See #15 above.

[30] Joe Lupo and Jesse Garza, *Life in Color: The Visual Therapy Guide to the Perfect Palette—for Your Clothes, Your Makeup, and You!* (Chronicle Books, 2008).

[31] Peter Walsh, *It's All Too Much: An Easy Plan for Living a Richer Life With Less Stuff,* (Simon and Schuster, 2006), 220- 221.

[32] "The Discovery of Inner Space," from a *A New Earth* by Eckhart Tolle, copyright © 2005 by Eckhart Tolle. Used by permission of Dutton, a division of Penguin Group (USA) Inc.

Additional Products from Lemongrass Publishing

To order more copies of this book, as well as other resources to help you organize, look your best and move forward in your life, please use this order form or visit us online. You can now order either digital books (by download) or printed copies, whichever works best for you!

Kathi Burns Presents:
How to Master Your Muck DVD
Watch and listen as Professional Organizer and Image Consultant Kathi Burns explains how to add space to your schedule, environment and wardrobe, so that you can become the master of your life and live your purpose!
Flash Download: $14.95
DVD: $19.95 (plus $3.50 shipping)

Essential Wardrobe Elements for Men
Do you ever wonder what clothing pieces well-dressed men have in their closet? Wonder no more. This checklist includes descriptions and advice about the essential items you need to have in your wardrobe.
eBooklet Download: $5.95
Booklet: $9.95 (plus $1.75 shipping)

Essential Wardrobe Elements for Women
A complete description of the wardrobe basics that every woman should have in their closet. Invest in these classic elements and you'll be amazed at the versatility within your wardrobe.
eBooklet Download: $5.95
Booklet: $9.95 (plus $1.75 shipping)

Freedom Filer Label Kit
Maintenance-Free Home Filing Kit - Deluxe Edition for households and home-based businesses: Freedom Filer's self-purging filing system will forever eliminate the hassle of cleaning out and reorganizing your files!
$42.95 (plus $6.50 shipping)

Freedom Filer Ready-Made Filing System
Take away the intimidation of having to set up a system for yourself. You can order a pre-made filing system and have it delivered right to your doorstep! Begin filing your papers immediately and start transferring files from your previous system whenever you're ready.
$139.95 (plus $36.50 shipping)

How To Master Your Muck: Get Organized. Add Space to Your Life. Live Your Purpose! (The Book)
Order copies for your friends, co-workers or business organization. Call for large quantity orders and discount pricing.
eBook Download: $12.95
Book: $17.95 (plus $3.50 shipping)

Sign up for FREE organizing and image eTips at www.addSpaceToYourLife.com

Qty	Title	Price
_____	Master Your Muck DVD	_____
_____	Elements for Men	_____
_____	Elements for Women	_____
_____	Freedom Filer Kit	_____
_____	Freedom Filer System	_____
_____	Master Your Muck Book	_____
	Subtotal	_____
	Media Mail Shipping	_____
	Total Enclosed	_____

Billing/Shipping Information

Name_____

Street Address_____

City _____

State _____

Zip _____

Telephone _____

Email _____

We will never sell or share your private information.

Return this form with your check or money order to:
Lemongrass Publishing
PO Box 232066
Leucadia, California 92023-2066

You may also place your order online at:
www.addSpaceToYourLife.com/Shop
PayPal and major credit cards accepted